ATTENTION

PLEASE!

ATTENTION PLEASE!

GAINING AND MAINTAINING THE ATTENTION OF CHILDREN IN YOUR TEACHING MINISTRY

JEFF WELCH

Attention Please!

Gaining and Maintaining the Attention of Children in Your Teaching Ministry

ISBN 978-1-7333289-2-0

Scripture quotations are from the King James Version of the Bible

Table of Contents

Dedication

To the first children's ministry worker I knew who understood the need to be an engaging teacher—my mother. I still remember how she would gather her children together on Saturday evenings to watch her practice the next day's Sunday school lesson.

She always included special teaching aids to help keep her young pupils' attention. I'm sure that she never felt like an expert children's ministry leader, but she was my first inspiration.

I love you, Mom!

Section I

Can I Have Your Attention, Please?

Many things go into an effective Bible lesson, especially when teaching children. But the content of your instruction cannot reach your students' hearts until you have captured their minds. You must earn their attention before learning can take place. The following chapters will help you understand the importance, types and enemies of attention.

Chapter One

The Importance of Attention

For forty years, he had cared for his father-in-law's sheep. It was a simple life, far removed from the pressures of the big city from whence he came. It was a quiet life: one that he relished. But this day, as he led his charges through a familiar valley, a flickering flame arrested his attention. 11

Fire!

Moses quickly surveyed the landscape for the best escape route. He must lead the sheep to safety. When he looked back to see which direction the fire was moving, he realized that it wasn't moving at all. The flame burned on a solitary bush; one that remained green and vibrant despite the heat. The sheep that had once dominated Moses' focus were suddenly forgotten. God had captured his attention.

Balaam's talking donkey.

Peter's vision of the sheet full of unclean animals.

A still, small voice to Elijah after the destructive wind, earthquake and fire.

Saul's encounter on the Damascus road.

These, among others, were extraordinary times of attention grabbing. One would think that just hearing God's voice sound forth from heaven would be enough to warrant notice. Often in Scripture, God dealt in such a way. But sometimes, He chose to employ unique techniques to gain the attention of His intended audience.

Smoke and thunder (and voice) from Mount Sinai were a sobering experience for the children of Israel. So was the sacrifice accepting fire from heaven on Mount Carmel. Daniel's three friends surviving the fiery furnace should have been a sufficient rebuke of King Nebuchadnezzar. But the vision of a fourth figure in the flames is what prompted his change of mind.

Attention is paramount in teaching. It is a prerequisite.

Focus

There are several types and multiple degrees of attention. If you talk on the phone while watching television, you might be attentive to both, but neither exclusively. Despite divided interest, you might follow the gist of each. But you would doubtless miss details of both. However, if you turned off the television and focused on the conversation, you would remember it better. Or, if you ended the conversation to watch the "how to" program, you might better be able to replicate the procedure being demonstrated.

When speaking at a college or seminar for the first time, I often introduce myself in the following way: "I've been asked to speak today because of my well-established reputation. Those who have seen me minister to children will testify that when I am speaking, children are always paying attention…to something—not necessarily to me."

With that, I begin to explain the importance of gaining and maintaining attention. The first goal of every session must be to gain the students' attention. There are many things you will do in preparation for the class period, but teaching itself will not begin until your students are engaged. They must become interested in some aspect of your instruction. There are at least three things that might merit their attention at the onset.

The Teacher's Draw

Do you have favorite speakers? No matter what the subject matter, you want to hear their presentations. Perhaps he has a soothing voice. Maybe it's an energetic personality. It could be that you are convinced of his sincerity. If you have a personal (positive) relationship with this person, you are more likely to have a natural inclination to listen. Whether it is personality, passion or something else entirely, something draws you to this speaker and you have no problem paying attention—at least, for a while. Of course, this attraction is born of previous encounters. Having heard or watched this leader before, you've determined he or she is worthy of your time and attention.

Thirty years ago, I was a frequent chapel speaker at the Christian school my sons attended. Admittedly, I was a little over-the-top with energy and methodology. The kids loved me. Years had passed when one of the ladies who taught in that school confided,

"When it was announced that you were the chapel speaker, the children cheered...and the teachers groaned. We knew that after chapel service, the kids would be so hyped up, we would get nothing done for the rest of the morning."

Okay, so I wasn't too balanced back then. The point is, some teachers are their own draw - and not just the exciting ones. Teachers who have a genuine relationship with students will find it easier to gain initial attention. You may have a calm and quiet demeanor. But if your students know you love them, you don't have to put on a circus performance.

Generally, when speaking to children anymore, I deal with crowds. Being a traveling speaker at Christian camps and church Vacation Bible Schools does not allow me to establish deep connections with my audience. If you minister to the same children week after week, you have the opportunity to build relationships. You can be the kind of teacher children want to listen to because you've demonstrated that you truly care about them.

Methodology
A second element of teaching that can capture attention is the methodology employed. How you present your material will greatly affect your students' attitude towards it. You can create interest in pretty much any topic with compelling methods of instruction. But if lecture is your go-to method, don't expect five-star reviews by your students.

When speaking to children who do not know me, the first thing I try to do is build a rapport. I might employ humor or entertain with a "magic" trick. If congregational singing is on the agenda, I lead it with enthusiasm. I want them to want to hear what I have to say. Once I've captured their attention with something of interest, I can move on to the Biblical truth I hope to communicate.

Much will be said throughout this book regarding teaching methods. Visual aids, music, drama, seat work, arts and crafts, creative writing, games, and more can be effective ways to gain and maintain attention. Capturing attention requires maintaining interest. Using a variety of methods is essential in this regard.

Some believe there is a fine line between effective teaching methodology and simply providing entertainment. It is true that speakers can overdo the attention-getting aspect of a lesson at the expense of valuable instruction. I have been guilty of spending so much time and energy having fun that I had to hurry through the content of the lesson more quickly than I should have. Still, how you present your lessons has a great deal to do with how they are received.

The Subject Matter
Another ingredient that could attract attention is the subject matter itself. We all have subjects we are naturally interested in. Given a choice between a healthy cooking seminar and a virtual tour of the latest and greatest cruise ship, I will always opt for the latter. Some Christians are intrigued by what the Bible says about prophecy, or finances, or family life, or witnessing. Mention a desirable topic and they may not even ask who is teaching.

In all honesty, it is less likely that children will be drawn to class by the mere mention of the lesson topic. Most children in ministry are captive audience members. They didn't come because they can't wait to hear about the subject at hand. But interest in the lesson matter can be cultivated through effective methodology and the teacher's passion for the subject.

Batter Up

As I stated, most children will not be intrigued by the subject matter. That gives you one strike before you even reach the batter's box. If you have not developed a relationship with your students that results in respectful attention, you've just swung and missed again. Don't be one of those teachers who just shows up. Don't teach just because you've been begged to, or because you've determined it is your responsibility. Teach because you love your class. Get to know them and let them know you. Build a bond.

If you've got two strikes against you, you must make sure this next swing connects. Present your lesson in ways that your students can't ignore. Become adept at using a variety of methods. Discover what works best for your students. Connect with them through how you teach. These three things are important to your learners: who is teaching, what you are teaching, and how you are teaching. Don't limit your potential effectiveness to just one area. Strive to create student interest in all three. Be a power player and hit each lesson out of the park.

Not only are there three basic tools you have that can attract attention, there are also three basic types of attention. Each has its value and place. Understanding differences between the three will inform your decisions about how to retain or regain the attention of your class. The next three chapters will provide you with a better understanding of them.

Chapter 2

Common Attention

The first kind of attention is the most naturally occurring. It is easily displaced by almost anything: an unexpected sound, movement in one's peripheral vision, the feel of something against the skin, or even a distinct odor. A professional educator might call this *passive attention*. I call it *common*.

Default Attention

Common attention is the default type. It is in force whenever we are not actively attending to something. Generally speaking, everyone is always paying attention to something while conscious. It may not be the focused effort of one of the five senses. Your mind can attend to a daydream or series of musings. Common attention reacts to the strongest stimulus, tangible or not.

A boy feels a puff of air and he glances toward the ceiling register. He immediately notices a spider lowering itself by an almost invisible thread. "Will it land on Carla's head?" he wonders. "Maybe if I blow it towards her," he muses. As he puckers his lips and blows the spider in the desired direction, he becomes acutely aware of an awkward silence. Several students and the teacher are staring at him.

"Brady is blowing Carla a kiss!" someone cries out. Laughter ensues. Class is over until the teacher regains attention. Distraction is the culprit. Common attention is the weak link.

Imagine that you have reached a climactic point in your life-related story. The entire class is leaning forward in anticipation. Without warning, the sound of a bodily function (you can choose which one) escapes a child in a bombastic way. This, of course, is followed by a litany of commentators providing their take on the incident.

If only this force of evil could be harnessed for good! It can be, and it must be. For as much havoc as it can wreak, common attention is one of the teacher's easiest-to-wield weapons. You can use your understanding about common attention to make it a cherished teaching partner.

Common attention tends to be at the mercy of the strongest attraction to the senses. That makes commandeering its benefits quite easy. All you have to do is provide the greatest sensation. But, you will need more than one weapon. You will need a stockpile of attention arrestors.

Stock Your Armory
Every good teacher's arsenal should include several common attention getters. Almost anything can be used as long as it has a relatively universal appeal to the senses. Remember, you are targeting one of the five senses.

ATTENTION PLEASE

Let's begin with the most commonly attacked gateways to the mind. In a classroom, most distractions are heard or seen. The most direct approach to regaining lost attention is through the ears.

Now hear this

A loud sound may be just what the doctor ordered. Keep in mind that you don't want your attention-getting sound to travel outside of your classroom. It is rather inconsiderate to regain your class's attention with something that distracts the students next door. The last thing you want is a "how loud can you get" contest with another teacher.

One tried-and-true noise maker is a bell. We old timers remember them as a common item on elementary teachers' desks. When attention waned, the teacher rang the bell to draw us back to her instruction. You don't see it as much anymore. Perhaps it doesn't carry the punch now as much as it did in my generation. But it is worth considering.

Of course, in larger groups or at outdoor activities, the use of whistles and bull horns is appropriate. I doubt that many readers teach Sunday school in a gym or on a football field. Still, if you take you class outside, you should plan on the appropriate equipment to communicate clearly, as well as to regain wayfaring attention.

Clapping is a common tool that is always at hand (pun intended). Two claps in rapid succession could stimulate enough curiosity to draw attention your way. Some attention getters like fingernails on a chalkboard, rubbing a balloon so it squeaks, and crying or screaming uncontrollably might get attention, but they won't necessarily create a desire to pay attention. The sounds you employ should not be particularly unpleasant.

Perhaps the easiest tool is a special word or phrase that you condition your students to respond to in a specific way. You have probably noticed that most public speakers use verbal cues to attract attention. Among preachers, those cues tend to be promises that the message is almost finished. "And finally," "In conclusion," "This, and I'm done," are among the lies frequently uttered in the hopes that listeners will perk up at the prospect of cessation.

Those particular phrases will have little effect on children. But the concept is correct. Speakers who minister to large groups of children use this approach. When the crowd gets restless, one man I know barks out orders like a drill sergeant. "Sit up straight and tall. Suck in your gut. Look straight up here." This seems to work in a large Christian camp setting. I try to have a word or phrase that fits with the camp or VBS theme where I am speaking.

There are ways to make the use of a special word or phrase more effective. First, explain to the children the appropriate response to your cue. "When I say 'Attention', you stand up, salute and call out, 'Yes sir!' Then, when I say, 'At ease', you sit down quietly." Expecting a specific reaction to your cue forces the students to focus on the activity called for. This helps draw attention away from whatever distracted them in the first place.

Professional educators are expert at regaining attention. They have to be in order to survive. Sunday teachers need only marshal attention for an hour or less. School teachers wrestle with attention deficit all day long. These teachers might say something like "To infinity…" Students understand they are to finish the phrase by saying "and beyond." Of course, there are a lot of secular phrases from which you can choose. But a little discernment will go a long way in choosing phrases in Christian ministry. Here are a few possibilities.

Teacher		Class
Flat tire	-	Shhhh
Hot fudge	-	Sunday
1,2,3 eyes on me	-	1,2 eyes on you
Zip it, lock it	-	Put it in your pocket
Jesus loves me	-	This I know
Slow to speak	-	Quick to hear
Shadrach, Meshach	-	And Abednego
Do right	-	'Til the stars fall
Class, class	-	Yes, yes

Another approach is to softly say, "If you can hear me, raise one hand." Those who don't raise a hand will likely notice those who do. Follow up with, "If you can hear me now, raise both hands." By this time, everyone is likely on board. You can add variety and fun by having the students duplicate your posture. "If you can hear me, do this" (strike a humorous pose).

You can increase effectiveness further by rewarding the most immediate responders. But it is not necessary to give something tangible to the first one who reacts appropriately. I suggest giving points away because they are free and always available. The first person (or the first entire team) to respond properly earns points or some other recognition. Older children love friendly competition. It doesn't cost you anything to give points to the boys' (or girls') team, but it creates a lot of excitement and helps draw attention back to the teacher.

The military example I described earlier takes a bit of time to enact. You might choose a simpler response like "sitting up straight." But standing provides the added benefit of letting the children move and stretch. This is especially helpful if much of the class time is spent sitting.

Interestingly, the absence of sound can also attract attention. Just stop what you are doing, stand still and watch the class. This should ultimately create an unfamiliar environment. Students gradually realize that a familiar sound is absent - the teacher's voice. They will look for you to see "what's up."

See what I did there?
Visual stimuli are also potent weapons in your arsenal of attention getters. They tend to be more subtle than audible cues. Perhaps you remember an early elementary teacher turning the classroom lights off to regain attention. Once the class responded properly, she turned the lights back on.

Another visual tool is teacher movement. If you tend to stand while teaching, take advantage of any opportunity to walk around. If your room is too small or you usually sit while teaching, make use of gestures. Movement can be either distracting or attracting. Use it for your benefit.

Another movement that serves as a cue is to get closer to and stand (or sit) next to a student or group whose attention is wayward. Your unexpected presence near the child's personal space is quite attention grabbing. Close proximity is effective in and of itself.

Of course, using visual aids while teaching is a helpful method we will discuss later. Here, we are just considering how to recapture lost attention by addressing the vision of your students. Any activity or movement can draw attention. Writing on a white board, putting a felt piece on the flannel graph board (am I dating myself?), holding up a picture, and tossing a soft object in the air (or across the room) are motions that draw the eye's attention.

Touchy feely and more
In the old days, a teacher could get away with a firm hand on a child. More recently, gently touching a distracted child's shoulder was still acceptable. Anymore, you must be careful of any physical contact. We are sensitive enough to feel a fly on our skin (or even on our hair). So, it would be nice to use this sensitivity to the teacher's advantage. While the sense of touch is an effective path to regaining attention, it is also the most personal. For that reason, take great care in how you attempt to gain attention physically.

The other senses are smell and taste. While these can be addressed while teaching, they have limited value as avenues for regaining lost interest.

Attack

When attention is waning, attack your students' senses in a way that's difficult to ignore. But remember, common attention is easy to regain because it is naturally short-lived. You cannot keep attention by ringing a bell or clapping your hands. You can only temporarily regain it. Something stronger than common attention must command your students' interest long term, lest you lose it again presently.

One other note: Overuse of any method can reduce its effectiveness. In fact, such overuse can become a distraction itself. Have a plan for regaining attention. Have several plans. As you become a better teacher, you will need them less frequently. But you will always need them. It is the nature of the beast.

Chapter 3

Compelled Attention

Common attention is fleeting, dictated by the strongest stimulus. An effective teacher pursues a longer lasting kind of attention. This active attention requires effort on the part of the learner. And effort is necessary if attention should result in learning. There are two types of active attention. Compelled attention is the term I choose that refers to the less desirable form of active attention.

In truth, compelled attention only demands that a student appear attentive—regardless of genuine interest. It is normally motivated by a perceived threat.

"Pay attention or else...I will tell your parents/you will not get today's treat/etc."

"Stop talking to your neighbor or else...I will move you to another seat/your team will lose points/etc."

"Put that toy away or else... I will take it until the end of class/I will put you in time out/etc."

Ideally, compelled attention would never be required. A great teacher teaching a great lesson using great methods should never have a less-than-perfectly-enraptured student. But, we don't live in an ideal world. Unfortunately, compelling attention is sometimes necessary. Children are sinners. And even the best teachers have to be stern at times.

Not Without Value

Attention and interest are not synonyms. It is possible to command someone's attention without gaining his interest. Result-oriented attention is rooted in interest. But, like the common kind, compelled attention has its place. What if you have a student who has no interest in taking an interest? What if nothing you do seems to attract his attention? Perhaps some thoughts from the book of Proverbs are relevant here.

"Smite a scorner, and the simple will beware." (19:25)

"When the scorner is punished, the simple is made wise." (21:11)

Don't hit the child! But for the sake of your other students, you may have to resort to compelled attention. Don't allow an obstinate young person to ruin the class period for everyone. If you have no way of removing a difficult child from the situation, presenting an ultimatum may be your best/only option. If the child complies, you will have created an environment where others can learn even if the "problem" child does not.

You have a class to teach. You must maintain order so that you can share what God has for them this hour. Try other, less hostile approaches to gain your wayward child's interest first. But there will be times you must resort to compelling a child's attention.

Keep in mind the limited value of this approach. Compulsion reduces likelihood of an enjoyable experience. The student may indeed sit still. He may even seem to appear focused on your presentation. But compelled attention only guarantees external conformity. While you drone on, he may be imagining your hair on fire—or worse. You might regulate his behavior without gaining his attention.

Keep Your Promises
When you do make ~~threats,~~ promises, don't do so in anger. And certainly, make no promises you are unwilling or unable to keep. If you promise to tell parents, then tell parents. If you promise to move the child to another seat, do so. If you promise to withhold some treat or benefit, keep that promise.

A broken promise will do more harm than making no promise at all. Once children know you will not follow through, every promise is an empty threat: hollow words. I have only had to speak to parents on a handful of occasions in my many years of ministry. Word gets around. Once I've met with a child's parents, the rest of my class knows I mean business. Keeping promises is the only way compelled attention can be achieved.

Another important point about effectively compelling attention is that the consequence of wrong behavior must be meaningful to the student. Common threats are loss of grade or standing, loss of privilege or reward, or possible discipline from an authority (usually a parent). Since we teachers have no recourse that includes traditional "discipline," we must usually invoke the loss of something good.

Some children are used to hard lives and broken promises. They sometimes respond to threats of "losing a treat" with an "I don't care" attitude. When you find yourself ministering to "hardened" children, realize that God has given you an opportunity to show His love. That doesn't mean you don't discipline. But these are children who might need for you to take special interest in them outside of class. You should seek to build a relationship with them. Do this for their good, not for any ulterior motive. But don't be surprised if the children you show loving attention to outside of class become your teacher's pets in short order.

If your ministry includes children whose parents are not a positive, spiritual influence, be patient. Be aware that unchurched children don't know how to behave in the "house of God." Frankly, many Christian parents don't raise their children to behave properly, either. I'm just saying, don't expect too much in the way of good behavior. Recognize the limitations of your students' maturity. You want to help children behave for everyone's benefit, but don't expect them to act like adults—that would be boring.

If you must resort to compelling attention, try to move away from the negative aspect as soon as possible. When practical, praise the child for good behavior. Try to find a way to engage him. Perhaps he can hold a visual or distribute supplies. The sooner you can transition a compelled child to paying attention out of genuine interest, the better for both of you.

Let me offer a final word about sternly compelling a student's attention. Just as with common attention getters, overuse is evidence of ineffectiveness as a teacher. If you find yourself making constant threats to multiple students, you need help of some sort. You might need another adult to assist with the unruly. Leadership might need to find another place for them to be during class time. Hopefully, all you need is to study the next chapters to improve your effectiveness in capturing attention.

In discussing common attention, we dealt with some subtle (and not so subtle) ways to regain the attention of a child who has become distracted. Compelled attention tends to deal with children who are more disruptive than distracted. I've devoted a separate chapter to important tips for you to keep in mind when dealing with discipline.

Chapter 4

Captured Attention

The best kind of attention is active but requires little effort. Common attention is easy to obtain but short lived. Compelled attention lasts much longer, but requires effort that would best be focused on learning/doing. Captured attention is both long lasting and easily focused. It is the best of both worlds.

I can force myself to remain engaged in something uninteresting of itself. If I can find a reason to pay attention, I am mature enough to make it happen. But can children? Not so easily. Which is easier for you to do, pay attention to something of interest or pay attention out of duty or necessity? The answer is the same for young and old alike. Attention given to something of interest is most ideal.

I can stand in an amusement park line for an hour waiting for a favorite thrill ride. Scarcely ten minutes goes by in a department store with my wife before my back begins to hurt, my shoulders droop, I'm sighing and fidgeting. Interest is key.

Consider a woman who loves to do counted cross stitch and someone else who enjoys building airplane models. The skill sets are different, admittedly, but both involve intricate finger work. Each can pass hours doing the hobby she loves. But if you have them trade projects, both may quickly express fatigue. Captured attention is freely given because the focus of attention is interesting to the student. As such, a master teacher finds ways to create interest in the lesson.

Why it is Best

Captivated attention is best because it resists distractions. Have you ever been so engrossed in an activity that you didn't notice someone (in my case, my wife) trying to get your attention? Sometimes it is the third ring of the phone or knock at the door that we notice. Attention can be so focused that what would normally distract us, doesn't. If something does manage to pry our attention away, we quickly recognize its worthlessness and set it aside so we can refocus on what really interests us.

Captivated or captured attention is the longest-lasting type of attention. Common attention is fleeting. Compelled attention lasts only as long as the threat is relevant, or the energy needed to force attentiveness is depleted. Captivated attention can last beyond physical fatigue.

Captured attention leads to better learning. It seems too obvious to state that we learn best the things we attend to with interest. Does that limit our class's potential for growth to those topics in which they are naturally or culturally inclined? Not at all. We can cultivate interest in almost any subject. But we must begin with bait that is the most likely to attract them. Once on the line, we must keep them interested so that they will learn.

WrestleMania

Get to know your students' interests. I recall a time I scheduled myself to substitute teach a junior boys Sunday school class for consecutive weeks. Most of the class had little knowledge/ experience in proper church behavior (did I state that diplomatically enough?). Having a "new" teacher, to them, seemed a great opportunity for testing the limits of decorum (or the absence thereof).

I noticed at least one of them was wearing a WWF T-shirt, so I asked if the guys liked professional wrestling. Most responded enthusiastically. "My son is a wrestler in high school," I said. "Would you like me to bring some of the medals he's won next week?" Of course, I conditioned my offer with them behaving during the lesson. I kept my promise and even figured out a way to include wrestling in the lesson. If you have the same class week after week, there is no reason you cannot ascertain some of your students' interests and incorporate them into your class time.

The Downside

Like other types of attention, there is a downside to the captivated kind. It does not lie in the limitations of the attention itself, but in the abilities and effort of the teacher. It requires getting to know your students. That means understanding the general characteristics, skill sets, emotional status and interests of the children to whom you minister. Age, gender, culture, and ability are important considerations in determining general interests.

Four-to-eight-year-old children might love puppets. Sixth graders might not. Boys may like rough sports. Girls may not. Younger children sing with abandon. Children whose voices are changing and who are more sensitive to peer pressure are more tentative about singing loudly. I've included some of my general observations about children elsewhere in this book. You would be wise to supplement that with real research.

Once you have a fair grasp on general traits, you must advance toward getting to know your students specifically. Take the wrestling shirt incident, for example. What if I had noticed the shirt and said, "How many of you like sports?" The answer might have been similar. But if I had offered to bring my son's golf trophies, the response could have been significantly different. These "rough" boys obviously enjoyed the theatrics of TV "professional" wrestling. I can't imagine they would have any interest in the "gentleman's game."

There are several ways to gain insight into your learner's lives and loves. One is to simply observe them and listen in on their conversations. Since children rarely filter themselves among other children, you can get a good idea of their likes, dislikes, personalities and such in the classroom. But you will fare even better if you observe them outside of the ministry.

Visit them in the home. Go to one of their ball games. Take the class on a field trip with enough helpers involved so you can focus on observing instead of corralling. Invite small groups to your home for snacks and games. Ask questions and listen to the answers.

Another way to gain insight is to take surveys. A written survey allows you to review the responses, but a verbal survey is more spontaneous. Children may not be able to spell the right words for a written survey. So, answers may be blunted. Still, I like written surveys because they tend to be more thoughtful and less influenced by someone else's answers.

Here are some questions you could include:

1. What is your favorite candy?
2. What is your favorite dessert?
3. What is your favorite main meal item?
4. What is your favorite TV program?
5. What is your favorite movie?
6. What is your favorite song?
7. Who is your favorite musician?
8. What is your favorite musical instrument?
9. What is your favorite type of music?
10. What is your favorite board game?
11. What is your favorite card game?
12. What is your favorite sport to watch?
13. What is your favorite sport to play?
14. How many "best" friends do you have?
15. How many other regular friends do you have?
16. What do you do with your friends?
17. How would you describe yourself as a student in school?
18. How would you describe yourself as a child at home?
19. What is your dream vacation?
20. What are you most afraid of?
21. What job would you like to have when you are an adult?

ATTENTION PLEASE

Another use for surveys is to discover what teaching methods your pupils might appreciate. Give them a list and ask them to rate them by putting the number 1 next to those they like a lot, 2 next to those they enjoy occasionally, 3 next to methods they prefer to avoid.

1. Puppets
2. Videos
3. Arts and crafts
4. Drama (teacher acts)
5. Drama (students act)
6. Maps and diagrams
7. Group discussion
8. Lecture (teacher does all talking)
9. Interesting stories
10. Question and answer games
11. Experiments
12. Music
13. Small group projects
14. Individual projects
15. Field trips
16. Puzzles
17. Object lessons
18. Pictures

Some survey questions are more revealing if the answers are anonymous. For example, have students rate themselves in the following categories. They can use an "A" for always, "U" for usually, "S" for sometimes, "R" for rarely, and "N" for never.

1. I am honest about good things
2. I am honest when I am wrong
3. I argue with parent(s)
4. I am happy at home
5. I feel safe at home
6. I feel safe at school
7. I worry about having food
8. I worry about bullies
9. I worry about school grades
10. I worry about not having friends
11. I worry about being bad at sports
12. I listen to music with sinful language and ideas
13. I watch shows/movies with lots of violence
14. I watch shows/movies with lots of bad language
15. I watch shows/movies with sex/nudity

Hopefully, this gives you some ideas. Of course you must be discerning about the questions you ask. You may want to have a church leader approve any list that might include sensitive questions. Naturally, you should not overload students with dozens of questions at one time. You could take a few minutes occasionally to get input on four-to-seven questions. Try to bundle questions according to theme.

As you get to know your students, you will discover that finding common interests becomes increasingly difficult with class member diversity. Boys and girls can certainly learn together. And combining them creates an interesting dynamic. But it also broadens the scope of interests. The greater the age span of your group, the harder it will be to find methods that interest all parties.

Some divisions should be avoided regardless of perceived benefits. Children from different cultures should be integrated, not separated. The stigma of segregation is more undesirable than the need to make teaching easier. Naturally, the exception to this is if the two groups do not share a common language.

Including your pupils' everyday interests in your lesson plan will help keep their attention. But there is a limit to how much superheroes can be incorporated into Bible exposition. You will garner a lot of information through surveys that does not help you teach. But it will help you know your students.

Parents and professional teachers are other sources of information. Ask moms and dads what challenges their children face, what worries they express, what they enjoy, and what they avoid. If you know any educators who teach your age group, ask them the same. Ask how children spend free time, how they respond to authority, what kind of friends they have.

Another thought about capturing attention deals with addressing felt needs. This topic relates more to teens and adults than to children. In truth, children are not so much focused on "needs." They are more interested in enjoying themselves. Still, if you know what problems children in your class need solved, you can create more interest in your lesson. Perhaps you can create, and then satisfy, some curiosity, solve some problem, or relieve some frustration.

In short, you can keep students' attention via their interests.

Chapter Five

Enemies of Attention

If maintaining attention was easy, anyone could do it. Unfortunately, enemies of attention abound. There are three main antagonists.

Distractions

The most obvious enemy of attention is distraction. Distractions interrupt focus and draw attention away from its intended target. Anything your senses can experience is a potential enemy of attention. These annoying interruptions remove students' attention from what you are saying/doing. Frequently, a distraction is a loud or unexpected sound. Though most distractions attack the ears, they can come through any of the other senses as well.

There are different ways to deal with distractions, depending upon the degree of lost attention. First, assess the damage. Are most of the students distracted or a select few, or just one? Chapter two offers tips to regain the attention of a large group. Using those tactics to refocus one or two children might actually be distracting to a mostly attentive group. When trying to reengage one or two children, you could get closer to them. You might call on one to answer a question or serve in some way (like hold a prop).

Some distractions are easily dealt with. As a pastor, I often taught the adult Sunday school class in our church auditorium. Every week, the Sunday school superintendent went from room to room, informing teachers that the class time was almost over. He did this by ringing a handheld bell. I realize that some teachers lose track of time. But I am not one of them. Besides that, I faced a large wall clock while teaching.

For several Sundays in a row, as I was winding up my lesson, a door behind me silently cracked opened. A man's hand, holding a bell, became visible to everyone except me. But I knew it was there because every eye was diverted. Then came the ringing; ding ding - ding ding - ding ding. Most teachers are jealous over the last few minutes of class. This is when you make application, call for decisions, or otherwise try to conclude on a significant note. The bell ringing did not help.

As the pastor, I had the freedom to tell our superintendent that the warning bell would not be necessary when and where I was teaching. Sadly, other teachers may not have felt free to be so bold. This is a distraction that was easily remedied for me. If you experience distractions that might be easily removed, discuss it with the proper authority to make appropriate changes.

Maybe your class can hear the church phone when it rings. Although this may be a rare occurrence, it distracts for quite a while because no one answers it quickly. Suggest that the ringer be lowered or turned off during your ministry hour. Maybe the calls can be forwarded to someone's cell phone (set on vibrate). If there is no other option, perhaps you could make a game out of it.

Suggest to the class that when they hear the phone ring, they stand in unison and quote a Bible verse like Psalm 118:5, "I called upon the Lord in distress: the Lord answered me, *and set me* in a large place."

To deal with distractions you cannot anticipate or control, be prepared with attention-regaining strategies as described in chapter two. Distractions are most powerful when students are not engaged in the classroom activities. So, give them a classroom experience that is more interesting than anything that seeks to distract them.

Disinterest
While distractions seem to be the most common enemy of attention, disinterest is probably the most powerful one. It is nearly impossible to pay attention to something that offers no interest to you. No matter how many times the teacher claps her hands, rings a bell or flicks the lights off and on, if the lesson is not interesting, the task of teaching is hopeless. Disinterested parties are easily diverted. Sometimes your hearers simply do not see the relevance of the lesson or find your teaching style disengaging.

One way to keep interest is to implement a variety of teaching methods during each session. Repetition with variety is a great way to reinforce Bible truth without seeming redundant and becoming boring. Begin with a "what would you do" question. Read the Scripture reference responsively (if the children are able). Tell a life-related story. Have some children act out the Bible account. Discuss how the memory verse applies to the lesson. Conduct a mock interview, asking children to rehearse details of

41

the Bible story. Have older children write a paragraph explaining what change in their lives should take place based upon the Word. Younger children can draw a picture that applies the lesson. Invite willing parties to read their paragraph or share a testimony. Have prayer time that includes children who want to pray.

Using a variety of teaching methods, especially activities that involve the students, will keep attention far longer than lecturing will. Another consideration is the typical attention span of your students. This depends on two main criteria: age of the students and degree of student activity involved. While commonsensical, the following examples have not been scientifically proven.

Age group	Teacher presented	Students involved
Preschool	3 - 5 minutes	5 - 8 minutes
Early elementary	5 - 8 minutes	8- 10 minutes
Middle elementary	8 - 10 minutes	12-15 minutes
Upper elementary	10 - 12 minutes	15-20 minutes

As you can see, younger children tend to need more frequent changes in activity in order to remain interested. That does not mean you must have 9-12 different activities each week. You just have to break up the schedule enough to keep them engaged. You can share the lesson itself into three short parts: introduction, details, and conclusion. Separate these three leader-led methods with short student activities like singing, quoting memory verses or review game.

Methods that involve the students can generally be carried on for longer periods of time than methods that are primarily teacher driven.

In short, there is only one way to solve the disinterest dilemma: Be interesting!

Discomfort

This third enemy of attention does not get the same press as the first two. It often goes unnoticed or misdiagnosed. Among the enemies of attention, discomfort is the silent killer. We recognize distractions when they occur. We realize when our students are disinterested. But few teachers consider the importance of disarming discomfort.

If you are uncomfortable, your body's response to that discomfort will fight for your mind's attention. Have you ever been frustrated by a small child kicking the back of your chair? Do you suppose they do that because they are evil? Are they trying to provoke you to wrath? Of course not. They are uncomfortable. Try sitting on a table for a while. It won't take long before you feel the urge to move (swing) your legs to help with blood circulation. Sit still like that for twenty minutes and see if your legs don't fall asleep. Not fun.

Few churches make it a priority to provide appropriately sized furniture for their children's ministry. They might purchase very small chairs for preschoolers. But many elementary aged youngsters are forced to sit in chairs with their toes hovering above the floor.

Resilient - not unbreakable
I know that children are more resilient that we old folks are. But that doesn't mean they are impervious to discomfort. In fact, their

little bodies will naturally resist it. When a position is uncomfortable, don't you move? It's not rebellion. It is self-preservation. Wrong-sized furniture is one way to guarantee discomfort.

Is the lighting appropriate (not too dim or too bright)? What about the temperature? Can all your pupils see clearly? Do they arrive hungry? Did they get enough sleep the night before?

Of course, not all discomfort is rooted in the classroom environment. Children may come to Sunday school a little under the weather. Sadly, some are even the victims of abuse or bullying. Teachers cannot expect to have a solution for every discomfort. Just be aware that not all fidgeting is evidence of demon possession.

Recognize the Enemy
Are the children restless? Make use of a method that requires movement. Are they tired? Don't just drone on. Employ a method that encourages their involvement. Morton Blackwell's observation is pertinent here: "The mind can absorb no more than the seat can endure."

Discomfort may not be as obvious as disinterest or distractions, but it is a legitimate enemy of attention. Don't allow students to become the enemy in your mind. Don't even allow the undesirable behavior to claim that title. Instead, find the root of wrong conduct and fight it with all your might and resources.

Chapter Six

Dealing with the Disruptive

Children will sin. That statement is as true as it is blunt. Proverbs 22:15 tells us that "Foolishness is bound in the heart of a child." No matter how good of a teacher you become, or how interesting the lesson topic, or how engaging your method of instruction, you will have distracted, disinterested and maybe even disruptive students.

For a teacher, the purpose of classroom management is to provide an atmosphere conducive to learning. Sometimes this is easily accomplished by simply refocusing the attention of the distracted. In chapter two we discussed some ways to regain attention of an entire class. You won't use those methods to reengage an isolated child or two. Instead, here are some helpful hints.

You can often get a child's attention subtly by walking close to or stand directly in front of him while teaching. Without drawing attention to him, your close proximity should refocus his attention. If that doesn't do the trick, you might gently touch him on the shoulder. This touch must not seem disciplinary, harsh or cause any physical discomfort. Be sure touching in this way is not restricted by your ministry's code of conduct or rules for discipline. If it is, skip it.

The next step could be to direct a question or comment to him. Say his name first to get his attention. This allows him to focus on your comment or question. Any question should not aim to address his inattentiveness. You are not trying to embarrass the child or put him on the spot.

If you need to get a child's attention directly, stop speaking and look silently at the misbehaving child. If he does not soon look your way, call his name with a serious tone and countenance. Give him specific instructions to discontinue wrong behavior.

One principle for dealing with a difficult child is to keep him off guard. When we treat people differently than they expect, it throws off their emotional equilibrium. Proverbs 15:1 is insightful: "A soft answer turneth away wrath: but grievous words stir up anger."

Children who have made a habit of disobeying or disrupting are accustomed to being yelled at or ignored. When you respond differently, it sets a new dynamic. Naturally, you cannot ignore behavior that distracts others in the class. Nor can you expect a positive response by losing your temper. (Two wrongs don't make a right.) So, here are a couple considerations.

Be gentle
Express kindness in spite of your displeasure. Pay attention to your eyebrows and lips. Our natural inclination is to frown at wrong behavior. Don't lower your eyebrows. Express surprise and slight confusion instead of anger. This shows that you expect better because you know the child can do better. Sighing instead of huffing also expresses disappointment instead of anger.

Assure the child that you believe he can do better. Even ask if there is something you can do as the teacher to help him behave (sit still, stop talking, pay attention, etc.).

Offer choices
Avoid ultimatums. When possible, offer a choice in solving a problem. Make sure both options are acceptable to you. Normally one choice is preferable to the student. Allowing the child to choose between two remedies is less threatening and has greater potential for compliance with a reasonably decent attitude.

"Can you quit talking to/playing with Ryan, or would you rather move to another seat?"

"Do you want to put that away in your pocket or let me keep it until class is over?"

Special attention
Many Christian teachers (and parents) are under the false impression that treating all their children equally is a Biblical standard. It is not. Being fair does not guarantee equality. Jesus did not give everyone He met the same amount of time and attention.

Even some of His disciples had more intimate experiences with Christ than did others.

Having favorites will certainly lead to problems. But treating some children differently is not necessarily favoritism. Some children need more attention. Some need more encouragement. Some need greater challenges. As their teacher, you must discern their needs and seek to meet them as your role provides.

Some "problem children" need extra positive attention. Let the child help in a special way. Perhaps you can reinforce better behavior by offering a reward system unique to that one child. Discernment is needed when opting for this approach. Other children can feel cheated or even encouraged to misbehave in order to get the same "deal." So, limit special treatment in scope, time and value. Use it as a temporary measure only.

Expect challenges. Stay on guard, and you can win the battle. Here are some helpful reminders to follow when dealing with the disruptive.

Rules of Discipline
1. Neither be, nor appear, vindictive. It is natural to become angry at bad behavior. But this is not the time to let nature runs its course. This is a time to be supernatural. Correcting a child is not about your offense. So, deal with problems with a calm spirit. Remember how patient God is with you.

This can be especially challenging since dealing with problems is not one of our favorite things to do. You will not be in an ideal frame of mind. So, you will have to make a conscious effort to be as pleasant as possible while correcting an issue.

2. Express disappointment in the wrong behavior, not anger at the child. Not to sound too psychological, but there is a significant difference between rebuking a wrong action and attacking a child's

motive or character. Behavior is easier to change than character. It is also easily measurable—you can quickly tell if behavior truly changes.

Rebuking a lie is dealing with the action. Calling the child a liar labels him in a way that he may come to accept as "just the way I am." Showing disappointment in a child taking something he shouldn't is more appropriate than calling him a thief. Dealing with the offense allows children to see the sin as a wrong behavior instead of a character flaw they may be helpless to repair.

Lest you think I am minimizing sin, let me state that sin does come from the heart. It is not just behavior issues. However, as teachers, we should leave the challenge to a child's character to the Holy Spirit.

3. Don't embarrass the child unnecessarily. There are subtle ways to deal with minor infractions. But some wrong behaviors require more direct correction. That being the case, minimize public correction as much as possible. Humiliating a child unnecessarily looks more like vindictiveness than loving kindness.

Few teachers have the luxury of a helper who deals with trouble or takes the class while you do. If you are so blessed, make sure your helper understands how to help you when a child's behavior becomes problematic. If you are alone, express disappointment more than frustration or anger at the offense.

4. Follow through on promises (threats). Yes, I've already covered this. But it is important enough that is bears repeating. One of the worst mistakes teachers make when correcting children is to make threats in frustration or anger. Don't do this. If you promise a consequence for a repeat offense, be prepared to keep that promise. Don't make promises lightly. Once you are known to have a worse bark than bite, your promises/threats become a joke.

5. Do not get physical except to protect against physical harm. This is an area where your entire staff should refer to legal requirements and expectations. Your church or ministry should have clearly defined guidelines regarding physical contact with children. As it relates to discipline, never manhandle a child or use physical force. I believe the only exception might be to carefully restrain a violent child in order to protect others (and perhaps himself).

There are good organizations like the Christian Law Association (christianlaw.org) and National Center for Life and Liberty (ncll.org) that can provide your ministry with valuable legal counsel. In this lawsuit minded society, you don't need to do something that creates legal problems for you or your ministry. Be informed, and follow the guidelines.

6. Praise a corrected child as soon as possible and appropriate. Once a child responds properly to correction, look for opportunities to praise good behavior. Affirm good choices in order to reinforce continued better behavior. Even the most ornery children appreciate praise. Depending upon the child, you can thank him in public or in private if he has at least tried to improve.

7. Always have a reliable witness. I know most children's ministries have a limited number of volunteers. But in this day and age, it is unwise to conduct a class without another leader or adult helper. This is especially true if the need for correction comes to bear. You should have someone who can honestly describe the event.

Purpose of Discipline
Discipline is not punishment. It is not Christlike to "get even" (or get ahead). We need order in the classroom so that we can minister to our students. We discipline in order to restore. Our goal is not to isolate or make an example of someone who misbehaves. But if the offender responds improperly, the discipline's main value might be as a warning to others. Our hope, though, is that loving rebuke will be recognized as such and result in three things:

Restoration
Matthew 18:15 and Galatians 6:1 make clear that the goal of godly discipline is a restored relationship. We want to bring the erring child back into fellowship with other students and leaders.

Righteousness

Hebrews 12:11 teaches us that the desired outcome of proper "chastening" is the "peaceable fruit of righteousness." We correct children to help them glorify God by doing what is right.

Self-discipline

Only God can change the heart. One of the tools He uses to form character is discipline. As a teacher, you participate in that endeavor by insisting upon correct behavior. But you should not be satisfied with simple compliance. Your hope is that correction helps your pupils develop self-discipline.

This is not behavior modification. This is loving leadership.

Section II

Methods

Your methodology includes the types of tools you use to communicate. These are your methods of instruction. Many published curriculums employ a variety of mediums and techniques to aid the teaching process. Ministry leaders who must develop their own materials should avail themselves of similar (if not greater) variety.

The more ways that you have at your disposal to communicate truth, the better you can engage the attention and interest of your students. The following chapters introduce you to some common, but valuable methods you can employ in order to teach more effectively.

Chapter Seven

Storytelling

If I had to choose just one teaching method, one way to communicate truth in an arresting way, it would be storytelling. I'd choose that for several reasons, chief among them being the example of Christ. As the Master Teacher, Jesus battled ignorance and antagonism. Storytelling was His weapon of choice. It is true that Jesus did not have some of our modern methods at His disposal. But I daresay He would still choose a good story over a Power Point presentation most of the time.

He was not alone. Scripture provides vivid examples of stories being used to drive the listener's mind to the speaker's intended destination. I think of Nathan's story to King David as an example. In fact, much of the Bible is God's story narrative of man's responses to God and the subsequent consequences.

Everyone loves a good story. Storytelling has been an effective tool for communicating truth and tradition since antiquity. Your improvement as a storyteller will correspond directly with your students' enjoyment of your teaching. No other method is as helpful, and perhaps necessary, in reaching both the mind and heart of your listeners.

Explanation

Storytelling is not just lecturing with characters and emotion. It is its own thing, its own world, its own reality. Storytelling envelops the listeners. It takes us on a journey to where anything is possible. It guides us to moral imperatives without being preachy. It reveals the consequences of choices without being demanding.

It is a safe place from which to see the mind of God, should the teacher dare use it accordingly.

Stories normally present a main character who faces obstacles to his desired goal. How he deals with those obstacles reveals his character. There is a climactic moment, often with a plot twist. Then good finally defeats evil. There is usually a resolution to most or all tensions created throughout the tale. Stories used in ministry should have an unstated, but clear moral message, a life application.

For ministry purposes, I suggest that there are three main types of stories: Bible accounts that can be told in story form, true-to-life stories that demonstrate real application, and fanciful stories that illustrate the main point of your lesson. My main caution is to tell Bible stories accurately and make sure children know that God's Word is the source. One way to reinforce this is to keep a Bible opened while telling those stories. Maybe even keep your notes on the open pages of Scripture.

Practical Instruction
Choose your story by first deciding its purpose in the overall lesson plan. Is the story intended to introduce the lesson, illustrate or reinforce a main point, expose children to the Bible text, or something else? Of course, you could come upon a story that is so good you want to tell it regardless of its relevance. Resist that urge. Set it aside until it is applicable. Or, change the rest of your lesson so that the story is relevant.

Get to know your story well. You shouldn't memorize it, but you must become familiar enough with it to tell it with confidence. If this is a struggle, try writing the story out in your own words. This activity will help you remember it and ensure that you can articulate it comfortably.

Create an outline of the story for practice and presentation. You might include the opening sentence, so you get off on the right foot. The bulk of the outline should be main points, important-to-remember facts, and perhaps transitions. If you are unsure of how to end the story, include a closing sentence.

All authors I've read about storytelling instruct readers to practice. This is good advice. For some, it is absolutely necessary. If this method is new to you, practice in front of a mirror. Or, better yet, record yourself and critique the exercise. In my experience, the need to practice wanes as you become more adept at any method. However, practice is never a bad idea.

When you do practice, don't just rehearse the words of the story. Practice all aspects of storytelling until you are comfortable with them. Practice out loud and visualize the story as you speak. I prefer closing my eyes during a first run through. Be mindful of appropriate voice fluctuations as well as body language and gestures.

Be aware of how much time your story will take to tell. Despite their wide appeal, stories can lose potency by dragging on. Take notice of the story's vocabulary and adjust it to match that of the hearers.

When choosing a story, ask yourself if it effectively communicates the desired message. Does it meet a need or goal, appropriately fitting the occasion and audience?

Presenting your Story
The first thing you must do when telling a story is connect with your listeners. Begin boldly and win your audience's interest. Use dramatic language, including action words. Speak loudly enough to be heard by all. Match your voice and body movement to the intensity of the story. Pause to create suspense or mark the passage of time. Give each character his/her own voice. Most

teachers can manage a variety of voices with simple manipulation. You can use a nasal voice, deep voice, baby voice, falsetto voice, whiny voice, slow voice, fast voice, etc. If you find it difficult to portray different voices, you can give each character a different facial expression and/or body position. Always try to speak a little slower than you do in normal conversation. This will help children follow the storyline.

Use appropriate gestures while speaking. It may feel clown-like at first, but your gestures should be more exaggerated when telling a story than during normal speech. Also, the larger your audience, the more exaggerated the gestures should be. When a character is speaking, express his personality. Even as a narrator, you should gesture to retain attention and express emotions.

You must communicate with more than words. Your face should mirror what the words are expressing. Your eyes and eyebrows are great tools for showing surprise, anger, fear, confusion, and more. Every tilt of the head and lift of the chin has meaning. Your lips can communicate even without uttering words.

You've probably heard that good storytellers, like actors, "lose themselves" in the story. I believe that is true. You must be able to set aside your inhibitions and become one with the story to be most effective. This is easier for some, but possible for all. I understand that telling stories to adults might be intimidating. But telling stories to children can be a delight. They will love you for it.

Age Appropriateness
Four and five-year-olds have very limited attention spans. Keep their stories short: four to six minutes. These children enjoy the familiar, so repetition is not necessarily a negative when ministering to them.

Less is indeed more with little ones. Use clear language with simple plots that are not obscured by symbolism. Stories should have very few characters and limited detail so that the children can keep up with the storyline.

Six to eight-year-olds enjoy a wider variety of topics. They have limited ability to separate fact from fiction. So, be careful to not present extra-biblical stories as canon. They appreciate simple stories of someone helping another or solving a problem.

Stories for these children can be a bit longer: five to eight minutes. While they can handle more detail, don't overwhelm them with trivia. Keep the story simple so the point is clear.

Nine to eleven-year-olds enjoy action and adventure. These kids love heroes, whether fictional or Biblical. They also enjoy biographies of real people. Because they are starting to grasp chronology and geography, your world of storytelling can widen significantly.

These pre-teens can appreciate novelty, irony, and plot twists to some degree. They enjoy guessing the outcome before the story ends. While their attention span is good, keep stories under ten minutes for best results.

Warnings
It is not likely that you would ruin a story. But you can limit its effectiveness. Here are some additional things to keep in mind when telling your story.

1. Don't use bad grammar or mispronunciation unless it is clearly character appropriate. Even then, use it sparingly because it can be distracting and/or incite laughter at improper times.

2. Avoid nervous body movements like clasping your hands or putting them in your pockets. Shuffling feet, rocking back and forth and fidgeting with a pen or glasses are signs you are uncomfortable.
3. Watch your posture. Whether seated or standing, you should remain above your audience's eye level with a commanding presence.
4. Make eye contact with everyone throughout the story. You might have been taught to look above your audience's head when giving a speech in school. But storytelling is more intimate. Look them in the eyes and draw them into the tale.
5. Know when to quit—then do. Tell the story, then stop. Don't moralize. Don't make application. Just quit. Let the story do its job. If the children are getting restless and you can't draw them back in, wind it up by skipping less important points.
6. Take note of the story's vocabulary and amount of detail. Change unfamiliar words to synonyms the audience knows. Eliminate unnecessary details and descriptions that might bog down the story.

Storytelling is a most wonderful and fulfilling method. But there can be too much of a good thing. You can use it liberally, but not exclusively. Telling stories can enrapture your students, but it doesn't allow them to be meaningfully involved.

Chapter Eight

Visual Aids

In the broadest sense, any part of the curriculum that is seen is a visual aid. Typically, visual aids are supplements to audible instruction. They can be images or actual items. They can be tangible objects or projections. Examples include the following:

1. Pictures or flannelgraph figures depicting the story being told
2. Charts, maps, graphs and diagrams
3. Whiteboards, chalkboards and flip charts used for images or writing
4. Overhead projections, slides, videos and computer presentations
5. Preprinted notes and checklists
6. Flash cards
7. Posters and bulletin boards
8. Costumes and props

Everything seen that relates to the lesson is a visual aid; anything that presents information visually. There is great value in utilizing visual aids. They help keep students' attention because more than one of the five senses is employed. Visual aids improve understanding by providing a second point of reference. And visual aids promote retention. Students tend to remember more of what they see than of what they hear. When those two senses are both involved, retention improves exponentially.

Practical Instruction
There are few directions to follow if you are simply displaying a single item or image. Namely, make certain everyone can see it and understands what the object is or represents. Often, several

items are used in tandem to aid in the teaching process. In that case, here are some tips to use visual aids wisely.

Be organized
Put everything in the order of use. Avoid the awkward dead space created when a teacher is looking for something. After any practice you do in preparation, place the items in order so that you can quickly identify and expose each at the right time, without delay. This means you should set things in place as much as possible before class begins.

Cheat sheets
Place a note with helpful information on the back of visuals is a good way to cue yourself while displaying them. While holding the item, you can glance at the info you've placed on its back to prompt you while keeping its front toward the students. You could also number the items to help you keep them in order.

Keep it simple
While helping at a Christian camp in Louisiana, I witnessed visual aids on steroids. The camp speaker was an accomplished evangelist with a good reputation for preaching to teenagers. This was his first foray into Junior camp, and he wanted to be well prepared. Well prepared, he was.

He had visual aids, object lessons, illustrations and other communication helps for every main point, sub-point, and rabbit trail point. I appreciate the use of visual aids, but this made me dizzy. He was aware of my experience in children's ministry, so he asked for input after his first presentation. I praised his ingenuity and passion to communicate effectively. Then I suggested he tone things down by reducing the number of aids he employed.

Using too many things might get confusing. Too much visual stimulus can distract from the message. I had a similar epiphany about "gospel magic." As a teenager, I began using illusions to illustrate Bible truths when I served as a camp counselor and in other venues. I quickly became popular among the kids. As an adult, I came to realize that gospel magic failed to accomplish its goal.

Children enjoyed and might remember the magic trick, but failed to recall the lesson it was supposed to illustrate. The method itself distracted from the message. The same can be true of visual aids. Only use the ones that truly help with interest, understanding and retention.

Show and Stow
Try to keep your stash of visual aids out of view when not being used. Then draw attention to each at the appropriate time. You might indicate on your lesson plan when to display items. Then hold or point to the visual you want to emphasize. You can even have younger children help by displaying them.

Keep items in view only as long as they help you communicate. Once an item is no longer needed, place it out of sight so that it does not become a distraction. A giant stuffed snake might be the perfect visual aid for your purpose. But if you don't hide it, children will have a difficult time ignoring its presence while you continue your lesson.

Age Appropriateness
It is important to use materials that are age appropriate. As you read this segment about each method, you will find common themes. These points bear repeating.

Four to five-year-olds need simple items and images. They tend to focus on one aspect at a time. If you show young children a picture of a zoo and ask what it is, they will likely point out the monkey or tiger.

ATTENTION PLEASE

Six to eight-year-olds will recognize that same picture as being a zoo. Still, try to avoid complex images or items that can be misunderstood. Maps, timelines and charts are not good tools for this age group.

Nine to eleven-year-olds are beginning to navigate more complex visuals like diagrams. I can't think of any limitations to recommend with this age group other than to avoid complex or technical images. Feel free to experiment. But gauge your pupils' reaction and their acceptance of the aids you use. Make note of the most and least effective ones and plan future lessons accordingly.

Remember, visual aids are tools. If using one doesn't seem fluid or applicable, don't force it. Just because something is cool, doesn't mean it will help you teach. Make sure the visual aids you use complement the lesson.

There are several methods that can rightly be called visual aids like puppets, object lessons, and games. Due to the unique qualities of some, we will deal with them separately.

Chapter Nine

Object Lessons

Object lessons are a specific type of visual aid. Their main significance is that the object is central to the lesson rather than supplemental. Object lessons are visual parables, comparing common objects to spiritual truth. An object lesson should focus on the parallel(s) between Biblical truth and the physical item (or what the item represents).

One advantage of a good object lesson is how the article attracts the attention of observers. These are great tools for older children who can think somewhat abstractly. Generally speaking, object lessons are easy to present. They can make complex ideas and concepts more understandable.

Warnings about Object Lessons
Coming up with good ideas for object lessons can be challenging. I have found many of the ones you can access online or in books to be inadequate as part of a larger lesson. Stand-alone object lessons as short devotionals are easier to come by. What are often considered object lessons could just as accurately be called visual aids. The main difference is the necessity of the object in the lesson.

It is easy to make improper or outright false parallels and applications. I have witnessed many presentations that failed to teach truth. I will offer just one example. A guest speaker poured water from a jug into a Styrofoam cup. He named the cup our heart (soul). The water was the Holy Spirit. He explained that the Bible admonishes believers to be filled with the Spirit.

He poked a hole in the cup with a nail that represented sin. He explained that sin causes us to lose the Holy Spirit. He proceeded to refill the cup while water continued to escape. He poked the cup a few more times and tried to keep the cup full with the picture of water. Of course, it was futile. He concluded by pulling out a drill and demolishing the cup.

Unfortunately, the lesson was not Biblical. Being filled with the Spirit means to be controlled by Him. It is not a matter of fulness in volume. And while sin does affect our relationship with the heavenly Father, we do not lose any of the Holy Spirit because of it.

Here is a better object lesson to teach about being filled with the Holy Spirit.

(Show a properly inflated basketball.)
"Do you know what is in this basketball? That's right, air. In fact, basketballs are design to function a particular way when they are filled with the proper PSI (pounds per square inch) of air. They bounce just right when they are filled properly with the right ingredient."

Bounce the ball. Then ask how the ball would act if it was filled with helium, water, or concrete. Explain that what the ball is filled with controls how it behaves. Can a basketball fulfill its proper function if it is filled with helium, water, or concrete? Of course not.

"God has designed us to be filled, or controlled, by the Holy Spirit. What are some other things we might be controlled by? The Bible uses alcohol as an example of the wrong thing to be filled with. People controlled by alcohol do not function as God intends. Anger, jealousy, and fear are other things we can be filled with or controlled by. If we are to fulfill God's purpose for our lives, we must be controlled by His Holy Spirit."

Another simple object lesson that teaches the Biblical concept of Spirit filling uses a puppet. Put a puppet on your hand and manipulate it for a moment. Ask the children why the puppet did the things it did. Of course, you made it do those things. Your hand was filling the puppet for the purpose of controlling it. If a child puts the puppet on, she could control it. Being filled with the Spirit means that we are yielded to God's control. We are obeying the Bible and letting the Spirit of God guide or control us.

As valuable as object lessons can be, they can just as easily be a detriment when used indiscriminately. Evaluate the application carefully. Just because you find a treasure trove of object lessons by a respected author doesn't mean they are trustworthy.

Application Limitation
Another caution I have is that you be careful not to draw a comparison out too long or dogmatically. Comparisons between spiritual truths and physical objects break down eventually. Some good examples are object lessons that illustrate the Trinity.

It is fine to point out that a three-leaf clover reminds one of the Trinity because it is one plant with three distinct leaves. Stop there, and don't try to make the point any stronger. The same is true of an egg. It has three distinct parts: the shell, white, and yoke. Yet it is one egg. A problem comes when you assign specific parts of the egg to each Person of the Trinity, like with water.

Water is sometimes likened to the Trinity in that it can take three forms: solid, liquid and vapor. Liquid is like God the Father. Ice is like the Son who became flesh (solid). Vapor is like the Spirit. There is a problem with taking this explanation so far. The same water can take any of those forms depending upon the environment. But the Father, Son, and Holy Spirit are not interchangeable.

Three matches held together and lit form one discernible flame (the Godhead), yet there are clearly three matches (individual Persons of the Godhead). However, if you separate the three matches, you have three flames (Godheads). You see, care must be taken to make basic points without exaggerating the parallels between the spiritual truth and the physical object.

Object lessons are valuable additions to your method toolbox. They are interesting and often insightful. Just be discerning. Choose carefully. Never compromise Biblical truth just so you can use a desired method.

Chapter Ten

Drama

You can choose from many methods of instruction that involve drama. Drama can be as simple as posing like the characters in a picture or as complex as a full-blown play with memorized scripts, stages, costumes and props. Some children love to participate, while others are intimidated by the prospect. Here are some brief descriptions of drama types you might employ.

Posing
There are two basic ways to initiate a posing activity. One of them is to show your group a picture/drawing with several characters. The image can be modern or Bible based. After assigning parts, discuss the picture with the class. Who are the characters? What is happening? With older children, you can explore what each person is thinking or feeling.

Next, have the children take their places. Look at the picture again and strike the pose. Each should imitate his/her character as perfectly as possible: body position and facial expression.

Take a picture.

A second type of posing is called Tableau. This strategy is often used by drama teachers. The main difference is that there is no picture to imitate. Instead, the teacher assigns parts and describes a scene to her "actors." They, in turn, must imagine their part. Some discussion beforehand might be necessary so that the pose is coherent.

If possible, create several poses that tell an entire story, or a key part of a story. Print the pictures and display them with captions.

Pantomime

A step up from posing is active drama without the characters speaking. Pantomime is usually associated with competition and guessing the character or activity being portrayed. You certainly can use it in this manner, but there is another way to employ pantomime in your classroom.

Choose volunteers to be characters in a story and explain their roles. As a leader reads or tells the story, actors portray the actions and attitudes of their characters. Students may not talk or make noise, but should use exaggerated gestures that are appropriate to their character and story line.

Set the actors in place before beginning. Briefly provide instructions, like what area to stay within. If possible, practice at least once before performing. When finished, discuss important and relevant topics with the class. What Scripture truths relate to this story, and how?

Full Drama

Performing a mini-play takes a considerable amount of time. It is worth it if your class enjoys this type of activity. If not, don't force this on them. Eager participation makes methods more effective. Depending upon the age and skill sets of your students, you should begin simply and gradually increase the complexity of your dramas.

Begin with very limited spoken lines. Let a leader narrate most of the story. This is a hybrid approach, moving from pantomime to full drama. Having limited speaking parts, children can concentrate more on their acting. As skill and confidence improves, graduate to more speaking parts and less narration.

Choose (or write) a Bible or life-related story. Assign roles and give scripts to the actors. Have them read through their lines twice. Then, walk through the actions. Practice the whole drama, offering suggestions for improvement. Don't be too picky. Have them practice once more before performing for the rest of the class or another group. As the class becomes more proficient, you might present your dramas to an adult audience.

One approach to consider is having all the students participate. With a larger class, you could have several dramas being practiced at once. Then have each group present to the entire class. This will take more than one session to prepare and perform.

If you do Bible dramas often, create some simple costumes for the children to wear while acting. The more authentic your drama preparation and presentation are, the more seriously your students will take it. However, we are not trying to train thespians, we are discovering Biblical truth.

Interviews
A dramatic interview involves one student acting as a reporter. He/she asks questions of another student who is assuming an identity (often a Bible character or famous Christian from history). You could have a list of questions prepared, or invite the class to help determine what questions to ask.

Prepare the person being interviewed in advance. Make certain he/she is knowledgeable about the person and events. If accurate answers are essential, you might have a leader play the part of the interviewee. The interviewer introduces the subject and conducts the interview.

Role Playing
Role playing might be out of reach for all but the oldest children. It involves students spontaneously acting out a situation that's been

presented. Describe a scenario and have the participants behave as if it is a real-life experience. Good role playing requires clear understanding of the characters' temperament and motivation.

Keys

Drama can be an effective teaching tool or massive waste of time. Much depends on the teacher's effort, preparation and expectation. Adhering to the following guidelines will provide for more desirable results.

1. Limit drama to a brief time period. There tends to be a lot of inactive (dead) time during practice. Don't let children lose interest and start entertaining themselves.
2. Make dramas extremely simple if children are participating. You want them to have a positive attitude about these methods. Their sense of success or embarrassment will greatly affect the value of drama in your ministry.
3. If a teacher or helper is a good actor, have him/her participate sometimes. A participating adult can help guide the children while being a role model for their performance and behavior.
4. Determine your goal for including drama, and evaluate its success. Why are you using this method? It may simply be to add some variety to your class activities. It could be to help children understand how others think and feel. Perhaps you are trying to build relationships among your students. Maybe the dramas will help children remember Bible events. Whatever the goal, ask yourself, is it working?

We've dealt with drama as a method that involves your students. Of course, you can also choose to showcase dramas presented solely by leaders. This approach can effectively communicate truth and elicit desired emotional responses. If you and your helpers are willing and able, present short dramas occasionally. They can be humorous skits or serious presentations. If serious, make sure enough practice goes into it, so the drama achieves its purpose.

Chapter Eleven

Puppets

Puppets are one of the oldest methods of visual entertainment. They are make-believe characters with real personality. Unfortunately, written instruction is not adequate in training puppeteers. If you want to become proficient, you should seek out some personal or video instruction.

One of the great benefits of puppets is the mass audience appeal they enjoy. We know that young children are easily entertained. But there used to be a popular prime-time television program with a cast of puppet-like characters. Naturally, the content and characters of a puppet show determine its audience appeal.

Types of Puppets
There are simple puppets, like stick figures created by gluing a shape or image on a popsicle stick. Finger puppets are made of paper or fabric. These are decorated as characters and placed on fingers for mini-performances (pun intended). Sock puppets are created with a sock as the body and head. These can be very simple or quite elaborate, depending upon the creative and detailed embellishments used.

Most moderately difficult puppets are three-fingered or big mouth. Three-fingered puppets are much older in style. They are full-bodied puppets with moving head and arms. You control them by placing the thumb in one arm and fingers in the head and other arm. Extra fingers are curled to fit inside the body.

Big mouth puppets are most common today. They have a big head where you place your entire hand. The thumb controls the jaw while the fingers keep the upper lip in place. Soft heads on smaller puppets allow you to disfigure the face, giving it a variety of expressions. Larger big mouth puppets have more rigid faces.

There are two types of puppets that require expert skill. Marionettes are controlled by a group of strings from above. Ventriloquist "dummies" are controlled by the human partner who "throws" his voice, giving the impression that the puppet is speaking. This puppet has more complicated controls for manipulating its mouth, head, eyes and more.

While styles of puppets may become outdated, puppets themselves are always in vogue. Currently, and for the foreseeable future, big mouth puppets are the popular option. You can easily find inexpensive ones. In most class settings, puppets with softball size heads are adequate. For larger groups, you will want to use puppets with heads the size of soccer balls.

Some puppeteers enhance their big mouth puppets by using a gloved hand as the character's. Sometimes this is done by sliding your hand through the shirt sleeve that the puppet is wearing. A two-handed puppet is possible if two puppeteers coordinate efforts. One controls the mouth while the other animates both hands.

Here are some good ways to incorporate puppets into your ministry.
1. The teacher can interact with the puppet(s) to introduce or discuss a topic. This can be more effective if students are involved in the conversation.
2. Puppets can serve as actors by presenting a skit or drama. There is no shortage of scripts available for puppet presentations.

3. You can allow children to control and talk for the puppets without a puppet stage. This kind of pretend play can give you an insight into the thinking of children as well as their ability to empathize.
4. Older children could put on their own puppet show. Provide an easy script to follow so they are not left to their own devices.

I suggest several guidelines for ministering with puppets.
1. Give each puppet a consistent personality and character. Puppets communicate by their known character as well as through their dialogue. Puppets with character flaws provide good examples of growth by slowly improving. As characters gradually "mature," introduce new puppets with fresh idiosyncrasies or character flaws.
2. Don't have puppets make spiritual decisions. Puppets should not pray. They certainly don't get saved. Puppets can discuss spiritual issues, but allowing them to make professions of faith places this serious decision into the realm of make-believe. The only exception is when puppets are portraying actual Bible characters in a Bible story.
3. Practice in front of a mirror. Synchronize mouth movement to audio. Move the jaw down, not the head up. Quiet, inactive puppets should face the talking puppet. Recognize your endurance limit. Managing puppets can be exhausting. Keep puppet skits fairly short.
4. Do not resort to ridiculous or violent behavior. Bad puppet behavior gets laughs but does not teach truth effectively. It only encourages children (especially young ones) to copy the wild behavior.
5. Build a puppet stage for ministry growth. Make it big enough for multiple puppeteers. Design it with two levels so that puppets can appear high and low. Plan it to limit arm fatigue. Your endurance will increase if you can stand behind the stage, holding the puppets just in front of you with your elbows relaxed near your sides. Of course, there needs to be a curtain between you and the puppets.

With the younger crowd, a teacher can use puppets without a stage. Just sit with the children, hold the puppet up and talk to it. Let the children talk to it as well. Use the puppet to ask review questions. Children won't mind the lack of professionalism.

Older elementary-age students will likely find the above approach "cheesy." You will want to have a more traditional stage for this group. While they realize that people are managing the puppets, they expect a more authentic production.

Puppets are also a great way for children to minister to adults. You can help them prepare a short program to present to an adult assembly, Sunday school class, worship service, or at a senior saints activity. When beginning this kind of ministry, use prerecorded audio. You could even have the children pre-record it. This will avoid challenges with the audience hearing the dialogue. Additionally, it will make the presentation easier for children to perform.

A puppet ministry does require some investment. But you can start very small and grow as the Lord leads and provides.

Chapter Twelve

Music

Music is among God's greatest gifts to man. Few things affect our minds, emotions, spirits, and even our bodies more than music. There are at least two Biblical purposes for music in children's ministry. The first is worship.

"Speaking to yourselves in psalms and hymns and spiritual songs, singing and making melody in your heart to the Lord." (Ephesians 5:19)

"I will be glad and rejoice in thee: I will sing praise to thy name, O thou most High." (Psalm 9:2)

"O Come, let us sing unto the Lord: let us make a joyful noise to the rock of our salvation." (Psalm 95:1)

"I will sing of mercy and judgement: unto thee O Lord, will I sing." (Psalm 101:1)

"Sing unto him, sing psalms unto him: talk ye of all his wondrous works." (Psalm 105:2)

"Is any among you afflicted? Let him pray. Is any merry? Let him sing psalms." (James 5:13)

Worship is the act of ascribing worth. That is, my worship exalts the worthiness of God to receive all glory and praise. Singing is a wonderful and beautiful way to express worship.

A second important purpose for music in ministry is exhortation. We sing about God to help others get to know and enjoy Him. To exhort means to build up. It is using music to and about God to lift up (encourage) others.

"Let the word of Christ dwell in you richly in all wisdom; teaching and admonishing one another in psalms and hymns and spiritual songs, singing with grace in your hearts to the Lord." (Colossians 3:16)

"And he hath put a new song in my mouth, *even* praise unto our God: many shall see *it* and fear, and shall trust in the Lord." (Psalm 40:3)

"Saying, I WILL DECLARE THY NAME UNTO MY BRETHREN, IN THE MIDST OF THE CHURCH WILL I SING PRAISE UNTO THEE." (Hebrews 2:12 quoting Psalm 22:22)

Music has a powerful way of affecting listeners. While the lyrics of a song are intended to present the main message, other ingredients like melody, harmony, rhythm and style communicate as well. Wise use of music is undoubtedly one of the best ways to minister.

Besides the spiritual value of music, songs can be chosen for practical purposes. There are several possible objectives for choosing particular songs. While I don't fancy myself a musician, I have written several songs that are used in children's ministry. Each was written with a specific purpose in mind. I have included the lyrics and melody of some as an appendix.

Some music effectively focuses minds on a particular theme (Psalm 101:1). Most of my songs were written to be used in specific ministries. "Kids For Truth" was written for a program with a similar title while I temporarily oversaw that ministry in a local church.

Some songs are great memory aids. I wrote "Armor of God" to help children remember the Ephesians 6 items in order. Bible verses put to music are especially effective in helping children memorize Scripture.

A song can teach a Bible truth or story (Ps 105:2). I wrote "Don't Quit" for a VBS program to briefly detail the interaction between Moses and Pharaoh. There are many songs that tell the story of a Bible character.

Setting the mood and mindset for the next part of the program is probably more easily done with music than with any other method. "Lord, Speak to Me" is a prayer song that gently moves the participants from an energetic program to an atmosphere that's ready for a Bible message.

Good music also helps children witness for the Lord. As children sing songs they've learned in your ministry, family, friends, classmates, and neighbors receive an earful about Jesus. This unintended consequence of music is enough reason in itself to make singing a big part of your work with children.

As powerful as music is, it can be rendered ineffective (or, at least, less effective) if the teacher uses it without discretion. Casual or careless use of music is an easy trap in which to fall. In order to make the most out of your music ministry, I suggest adhering to the following tips.

1. Explain words and concepts as needed. As a child, I sang the song, "Bringing in the Sheep" for many years. Yes, I noticed that some folks mispronounced "sheep," but it never occurred to me that I was the one in error. The Bible talks about sheep, so sheep was the most fitting word for the song. One day, in church, I noticed that even the hymnal got it wrong. What are "sheaves"?

Anyway, once I understood the song, it had greater significance to me. In case you are wondering, yes, now I sing "Bringing in the Sheaves."

2. Use songs with actions to help children expend pent-up energy. Besides the benefit of letting children get the wiggles out, action songs also help children remember the lyrics of the song by associating movement with the words. This tool is especially beneficial in learning Scripture songs.

3. Share your personal appreciation of special songs. Some songs and/or their authors have touching stories that make the lyrics more meaningful. When appropriate, allow children to offer testimony about a favorite Christian song that you use.

4. Don't forget to include older music, especially hymns. Maybe I'm an old fogey, but I am saddened that many churches are moving entirely away from older songs of the faith. I know that all songs were once new and that there are some great songs being written that are more up to date. Still, let me encourage you to not leave behind the music that carried the heart of our faith to this point. Teach kids a few good hymns. Let them sing those old songs for the older generation in your church. The senior saints will love it.

As with anything as powerful as music, there are some cautions you must take note of. First, only use songs that are doctrinally correct. Children assume the songs you sing accurately reflect the Scriptures. It is just as wrong to sing songs that are Biblically inaccurate as it is to lie to children during a Sunday sermon. Don't sing songs just because they are popular. Evaluate the message and only use those that teach truth.

A second caution is to avoid music styles and accompaniment that obscure the message of the song. If you have to read the words somewhere in order to understand what the lyrics are, there is something wrong with the music. Some music bids you bob your head or tap your feet. Other music begs you to shake your shoulders and hips. Consider what effect the music has on your body and determine if that is movement that glorifies God, or just pleases the flesh. I'm not telling you what music to use. I'm just saying that it matters.

Music can be used many ways in ministry. Antiphonal singing has one group of children singing, followed by a second group. This is done as if singing to each other. Singing in rounds also requires at least two groups. In this case, subsequent groups sing the same thing as the previous one, only a designated number of measures behind. Having a children's choir is a wonderful way of developing musical skill and knowledge. It is also a ministry opportunity. You can take your prepared choir to sing at nursing homes, adult services, and special events.

Worship and teach with music. There is nothing else like it.

Chapter Thirteen

Art, Crafts & Seat Work

Often relegated to "let's fill some time" busy work, seat work and projects are underutilized and under-appreciated as teaching aids. But wisely adopting these methods can greatly enhance your classroom's learning experience. Children love creative activity.

Arts and Crafts

Crafts are normally uniform projects. While there is often some room for individuality in design or decoration, everyone follows the same general instructions to create similar results: a plaque, wallet, bookmark, mug, picture frame, pencil holder, etc. These are great projects for emphasizing a specific aspect of the lesson they are supposed to supplement. Another benefit of crafts is that they all turn out pretty much the same.

Art projects are usually more subjective. Everyone might be manipulating the same medium by painting, drawing, modeling clay, or gluing toothpicks. But they have more freedom to choose what they paint, draw, mold or build. This affords participants some artistic liberty and allows them to more fully engage their imaginations and apply their skills. There can be great variance in the aesthetic quality of finished products within the same group of children.

Effective arts and crafts require several things. First, it is imperative that the project be intimately related to the lesson. Simply distributing coloring books and crayons does not qualify.

Ask yourself, "In what way does the chosen activity introduce, explain, illustrate, or reinforce the lesson?" Busy work might be enjoyable, but it isn't efficient. If you are going to use art as a teaching method, think it through.

Second, it requires preparation. You must determine what resources are needed, and make sure they are available. You need to plan how to succinctly explain the project, efficiently distribute resources, store finished projects, and quickly clean up. Part of preparation is thinking through whether the children can accomplish the intended assignment. You do not want it to be too difficult or too easy. How will you help those in need? How can you make it more challenging to the more capable?

Third, arts and crafts demand patience and self-control—on you part. You must let children do the work. It is easy to get impatient with stragglers and jump in to help. That is counterproductive. Instead of hurrying children who are slower, have additional instructions available for students who perform quickly. Some children are intimidated by hand work. They would rather sit by and watch you do it for them, so it is done (and looks) right. You can help by making suggestions. Encourage these children when they make even simple moves. This will help build their confidence.

With today's technology, it is easy to find ideas, examples and instructions for making use of arts and crafts. Here are a few topics you can research:

Drawing/coloring/painting
Posters/collages
Clay modeling
Finger or hand puppets (with paper bags, socks, gloves, felt, etc.)
Mobiles and other displays
Map making, Timelines, Charts
Macramé & Jewelry making

Sand art
Candle making/decorating
Soap carving
Models
Building with popsicle sticks, toothpicks, marshmallows, etc.

Seat Work

Another useful tool you should not neglect is seat work. This activity usually consists of completing an assigned project on paper. Though usually done individually, some seat work assignments can easily be geared for small teams (2-3 people) to complete together.

Like arts and crafts (and any method), seat work must be closely associated with the lesson in order to be valuable. It is easier to do so with this kind of assignment. Seat work can be used as a lesson introduction, reinforcement or review activity. Some types of seat work assignments are listed below.

1. Crossword puzzles give clues to words related to the lesson. The words fit vertically or horizontally in a chart. Some answers share letters. This helps the child verify one or both answers.

2. Word searches provide a list of lesson-relevant words that are hidden in several rows of letters. Circle all the words you find. They can be horizontal, vertical or diagonal. Harder puzzles might place the words in backward (d r a w k c a b) order.

3. Coded puzzles challenge children to use a code provided or a system explained to decipher a message. The numbers 1 through 26 might represent corresponding letters of the alphabet. Icons related to the lesson could do the same. Pictures might provide the clue. (A picture of an eye is translated as the word "I," the letter "u" as the word "you," and the letter "r" as the word "are.")

4. A case study provides a scenario. Students write a couple of sentences explaining the appropriate Bible principle that should be applied to the situation.

5. Word substitute puzzles instruct the children to write a synonym above highlighted words to help the students evaluate the meaning of the passage. In essence, they are creating their own paraphrase of the verse or passage.

6. Creative writing offers a premise for which pupils complete a story that includes an element of that day's lesson. You might suggest or require that certain elements or characters be included in the short story. You could ask students to write about how they have applied (or will apply) specific truths.

Of course, seat work can be as simple as a coloring page or completing a dot-to-dot project. The two most important ingredients are that they relate directly to the lesson and are age appropriate. Many published curriculums supply seat-work projects on a regular basis.

Learning Centers
Learning centers are small stations within the classroom where children perform an activity. Most of the projects fit within the categories of arts & crafts or seat work. The teacher sets up three or four tables with the appropriate materials for the chosen activities. Children can choose which activity interests them and go to that table to work. Teachers might limit children to one learning center during the class time, or allow them to visit more.

Purposeful arts, crafts and seat work are great ways for children to express themselves in meaningful ways. The downside of this method is that it uses valuable class time for what might seem like very limited teaching value. This is a fair observation. That is why I have emphasized making certain that your chosen activity be closely related to the lesson.

Chapter Fourteen

Group Discussion

There is little doubt that discussion is a valuable teaching tool among teenagers and adults (if you can get them to participate). But few teachers of children ever consider the idea. By discussion, I am not referring to a series of questions that children answer. Questions and answer sessions tend to seek short answers to *who*, *what* and *when* questions. A discussion includes *how* and *why* questions.

Because discussion as a method requires a base of knowledge and/or some critical thinking skills, it is more likely to find success among older elementary children. But teachers of younger children should not be afraid to try a modified version. The process achieves at least two purposes.

First, the teacher gets an opportunity to evaluate the thought process and attitudes of students. Second, children benefit from personal involvement and more engagement with the subject at hand. Both provide greater potential for real learning. As children state their understanding of a topic, and listen to others' thoughts (besides the teacher's), they are more likely to modify or moderate their opinions appropriately.

Discussion is not an exercise in debate or a contest to see who knows the most. This method presents students with a problem to be solved or a question to be answered. While the question might have a "matter of fact" answer, the emphasis of the discussion should be to determine the appropriate application of that information.

Provide a scenario about a problem that children face. Include three Bible verses that could possibly relate. Discuss how each passage might apply to the situation. Then, have each child choose the Scripture that seems most pertinent. You could reverse the order and have children make their choice before discussing the passages. Then see if the discussion changed any minds.

Here is an example: Justin was playing with his friend Chris when the two started throwing rocks at tin can targets. Chris pointed at a beehive in a tree and suggested trying to hit it. Justin wisely discouraged the activity, but Chris hurled a rock anyway. It missed the beehive and broke a window in the house behind it. The owner was already outside and immediately looked up to see the boys. Chris quickly pointed toward an alleyway, then ran to the homeowner and said he saw some teenagers throwing rocks.

"They ran that way," Chris asserted, pointing toward the alley.

"Is that what happened?" the man asked Justin.

What should Justin do/say?

What does the Bible say?
"A friend loveth at all times..." (Proverbs 17:17)
"...he that is of a faithful spirit concealeth the matter."
(Proverbs 11:13)
"A false witness shall not be unpunished..." (Proverbs 19:9)

You can discuss each verse to determine meaning and appropriate application. Then, determine what Justin should do and why.

Preparation

One key to effective discussion is your preparation for the activity. A big part of that is deciding what you hope to accomplish and how to frame your questions or present a problem. You don't want to present questions and problems with cut-and-dry solutions. At the same time, presenting overwhelming problems will be defeating and discouraging. Finding the right balance for your class is important. Better to start simply and determine their abilities, then increase the complexity or difficulty accordingly.

You do want your class to be capable of discerning a Biblical solution. You are not trying to stump them, but the discussion needs to be deep enough to exercise their minds and spirits. Plus, questions and problems must relate to their young lives in order for discussion to be valuable for their spiritual development.

You might talk about a Biblical account and let the children suggest alternative choices the character(s) could have made and the likely consequences. Eventually, though, you need to guide the discussion to personal application. This is where preparation is essential.

While the discussion should come across as rather free flowing, you have determined a target you want the children to hit. It is kind of like a magician's force. He makes you think you are making a free will, random card choice, but he is actually controlling the whole thing. You want the children to discuss freely. But you need to know where you want them to end up. You need to guide them to the finish line.

Limitations and Challenges

The first challenge to conducting a discussion is getting all the students to speak. You might need to implement this method in steps. Take discussing a Bible verse, for example. One week you might ask children to offer a synonym for significant words. The next time you use discussion, you could do the same but have the class talk about which synonyms are best. A subsequent effort should include actual discussion about the meaning of the verse as a whole. Once your class becomes comfortable with discussion as a class activity, you can move on to more thought-provoking conversations.

Another challenge is just the opposite of the first. That is curtailing the eager expressions of those few who love to talk. There are some extroverts in almost every group of children. You will need a plan for keeping them in check. One suggestion is to have a soft object like a ball or stuffed animal that serves to identify the proper speaker. Only the person with the token in hand (and the teacher) is allowed to speak.

Discussion among children will necessarily be limited to the knowledge and experience of the class. There is little value in a bunch of people speaking about something they know little about. Twenty minutes of discussion can easily result in no valuable information or instruction being offered, and no practical benefit to the class. For this reason, you must guide the activity. You may need to offer significant input to keep students on track.

I hope the magician's force illustration earlier did not come across as too manipulative to you. The fact is, as the teacher, you are responsible for the teaching result. Guided masterfully, the discussion method allows children exceptionally meaningful involvement that results in better retention and commitment to the result.

Chapter Fifteen

Review Games

Games can be used in a number of ways and for a variety of reasons. Active games offer opportunities for children to exercise and release some energy in a constructive way. Game playing can build camaraderie among players and even observers. Some games even help improve certain skills. But the most valuable purpose for games in ministry is testing and reviewing.

Review games normally don't involve typical sports activities. Instead, they tend to be question-and-answer contests that reward, or at least acknowledge, the team or individuals who best remember and understand the lesson(s) to which the questions refer.

Why use review games?

Games are fun for the children. Fun creates interest which improves attention. When used effectively at the end of class, children should leave with a positive attitude. Games are great tools for review because they not only test memory but also reinforce key lesson material. In addition, wrong answers to questions can be addressed to correct misconceptions.

Review games can involve many, if not all, the students. Even if only a few of the children participate, they should represent a team so that even those not answering will pay attention to the question and answer. Since spectators do not benefit as greatly as participants, wise teachers involve as many pupils as possible.

Teachers can evaluate the effectiveness of their teaching by the level of success students achieve answering review questions.

Good teaching is reflected in correct answers. Weak teaching is reflected in wrong/poor answers. Here are some keys to effective use of review games.

Make the process fun - be excited! Reward correct answers. You don't have to give away tangible prizes that cost money. In fact, be careful about those kinds of awards. You don't want prizes to become the focus of this method. I like to just give points. Since points are free, give lots away. One thousand points for an answer is far more exciting than ten.

Keep the game time short. Don't let the children lose interest. It is better to stop with the children wanting more than to play to the point of disinterest. Since the purpose of these games is review, it should not absorb too much of your class time.

Be fair. Do not manipulate the outcome. You may have to change the reward structure if one team gets far ahead of the other. But it is dishonest to change the rules or points so much that the team that should win ends up losing. That is discouraging to the losers and will negatively affect your testimony.

Try to balance the skills of the teams. Dividing the class between boys and girls is probably the most common way of structuring teams. Another common practice is to designate one side of the classroom as one team and the other as their opponents. However you determine teams, take note of whether one tends to fare significantly better than the other. If so, try to make the teams more balanced next time.

Have simple and clear instructions. Since game time should be short anyway, you shouldn't lead games that require a lot of time to explain. Complicated rules reduce the pleasure of playing. Fortunately, once a game is played, it takes less time to explain it the next time. Along these lines, make sure your game play features lots of questions.

ATTENTION PLEASE

One children's ministry leader plays a review game fashioned after the TV gameshow, "Who Wants to be a Millionaire." The game included iconic ingredients like "Ask the Audience", "50/50", and "Phone a Friend." The build up and play of the game was entertaining. This is fine if the goal is simply to have fun.

Because this approach results in just one or two children answering a few questions, it is ineffective as a review game since is. Great review games emphasize the questions over the game dynamics.

Perhaps the most important rule of thumb is to use good questions. Too often, review games focus on trivia. Sometimes they feature trick questions. This defeats the purpose. If you want these games to provide review, you should ask relevant and significant questions. Most teachers can't do that spontaneously.

Write questions in advance. Review valuable content or application. Ask questions that require the thoughtful response of a full sentence. Questions that can be answered with one word rarely reveal the depth of someone's understanding. Make sure questions are clear with specific answers.

Always make sure that everyone hears the correct answer.

Like every method discussed in this book, you can find ideas and instructions for good review games on the Internet.

Finally, a word about competition. Young children do not enjoy competing as much as older children do. And some church leaders believe that competition is not consistent with Christian ministry. You can include review games without the competitive element. The entire class can act as one "team" striving to reach a goal by correctly answering enough questions. Competition is not the purpose of review games. Reviewing the lesson is.

Chapter Sixteen

Take-Home Assignments

Most children's workers are familiar with take-home papers. These are usually projects (normally, coloring pages) that children begin in class and take home, finished or not. Teachers often suggest that students complete unfinished pages at home, but hey usually end up in the trash. This is not what I mean by take-home assignments.

Real take-home projects are designed to reinforce a lesson or to document activity related to the lesson. They are intended to encourage life application. Effective take-home assignments must be closely linked to the lesson content. They should guide pupils in meaningful activity.

Devotional Aid
Six short daily devotions can easily fit on a letter-size sheet of paper (using front and back). Instruct children to complete one block every day, Monday through Saturday. Each day's devotion includes a verse or short passage to read, followed by an assignment. The assignments should be varied. For example:

Monday - Children answer three relevant questions about the Bible text.
Tuesday - Have a verse printed with significant words underlined. Children write a word above each underlined word that has the same meaning (a synonym).
Wednesday - Suggest some practical action children can take. Children should have a witness sign the paper indicating that the action was done or attempted.

<u>Thursday</u> - Children write a brief explanation of the passage and how they plan to apply it that day.

<u>Friday</u> - Children write a note to God about how they feel about the devotional subject at hand. Encourage them to then read it to God as a prayer.

<u>Saturday</u> - Complete a fun puzzle with answers that reinforce the week's topic.

Start Simply
Children who are not accustomed to doing daily devotions will find it almost impossible to remember to take time every day for these assignments. If you want to start more simply, you might assign one activity they should attempt during the week.

These assignments can be as simple as typical seat work projects. Another approach is to suggest an activity that benefits others. Again, there should be a place on the page for a parent to sign, indicating the child's effort. An additional benefit to requiring a witness is that the parents can be involved.

As you move toward a more devotional approach, begin with three sections instead of six. Instruct children to complete the first one on Monday or Tuesday, the second one on Wednesday or Thursday, and the third on Friday or Saturday.

Self-Evaluations
Another simple way to include take-home assignments is to simply have the children indicate how successful they were at applying the week's lesson. Let's say you've taught about anger. On this week's sheet, have seven partial faces drawn. Label each with a day of the week, beginning with Sunday. The identical faces could be a circle with simple eyes and a nose. At the end of each day, children finish the face by adding a mouth (and maybe eyebrows) to indicate what their temperaments were that day. You could have sample faces drawn with captions to help them correctly reflect their mood.

Admittedly, this is very basic, but it is a start. It is better to begin simply and grow in complexity than to demand more than children are willing to do. Which brings us to a salient point: Children hate homework. Most youngsters make no effort to complete take-home projects.

I know.

Of all the methods, this may be the most difficult to include. And yet, if the goal is for children to apply each Bible lesson to their lives, take-home projects offer the greatest potential for success. While you will likely always struggle to get a majority of your class to participate, here are some suggestions to encourage cooperation:

1. Keep the assignments simple, with limited time commitment.
2. Find ways to make the assignment fun or interesting.
3. Require that assignment sheets be returned to class.
4. Acknowledge those who return their completed assignments (perhaps with a chart).
5. Reward those who consistently participate with a special prize or activity.
6. Involve parents by keeping them informed of your plans and purpose.
7. With today's technology, you should consider sending daily or occasional reminders.

Take-home projects are not for the faint of heart. It takes some time for children to get into the habit of completing them. With proper planning and patience, you should find that take-home assignments are worth the effort.

96

Section III

Be Ye Doers

In section one, we emphasized the importance of gaining and maintaining the attention of our students. Learning cannot begin until attention is arrested by way of capturing students' interest.

Section two introduced you to a variety of tools that will make keeping attention easier and teaching more effective. I encourage you to make every effort to include many of these methods in your teaching.

Finally, section three offers insight into the general characteristics of the children in your ministry which will help you determine what methods are best for your students.

Chapter Seventeen

Choosing the Right Methods

There are two basic types of teaching methods. Each has its strengths and challenges. Direct instruction is any method that points attention to the teacher. The greatest value of direct instruction is that lots of information can be communicated accurately because the lesson material is prepared and presented by the person with the most knowledge of the subject. One weakness is, without participation or effective motivation, students have a difficult time being attentive to the lesson. Secondly, teachers who do all the talking cannot know if the students are truly learning.

Other types of teaching methods fall into the category of indirect instruction. These require active participation from the students. The obvious strength is that students retain much more of the information they discover themselves because their interest is heightened by involvement. One challenge with indirect instruction is that less lesson material is introduced because indirect instruction is limited by the skills and knowledge of the students. Teachers must be prepared to guide activities and lead students to Biblical conclusions.

The major reason to employ various teaching methods is to retain student interest so truth can be presented, accepted and remembered. Here are some winning strategies in maintaining attention:

ATTENTION PLEASE

1. Stimulate thinking by asking questions and assigning projects.
2. Involve the students as much as possible.
3. Teach to multiple learning gates (senses).
4. Make the learning experience pleasant. Be happy; your attitude rubs off.
5. Provide ample opportunities for success, and encourage your students often.

Once you have several teaching methods from which to choose, how do you determine the right one? Or, does it even matter? Yes, it matters. A carpenter has many valuable tools that aid his efforts, each with its purpose. You could pound a nail with the handle of a screwdriver, but a hammer is more effective. You could cut through a piece of wood with a chisel, but a saw would be faster and provide a cleaner edge.

Having choice methods available is beneficial. Using the right ones at the right times is wisdom. Let's rehearse some of the factors you should consider when deciding upon a method for teaching the truth at hand. By considering the answers to all these factors together, you will be able to narrow your options.

First, what is the age range and gender of your students? Age will determine their attention span, cognitive skills, and physical abilities. When considering a method, ask yourself these questions: Will this method keep their attention? Can they effectively do what needs to be done? Will they grasp the point and understand the lesson?

At younger ages, gender is less of an issue. With older pre-teens, the difference between girls and boys is more pronounced. Not so much in ability, but in interest. You should keep that in mind when choosing methods.

Second, consider the size of your group. Some methods are more easily geared to small groups while others require more participants in order to be effective. For example, if you want to have the boys play a traditional sport, a small group of six could form two teams for basketball. But you would need eighteen to play baseball. Are there enough children to do this activity effectively? Are there too many children to do this right? Uninvolved students could easily get bored.

Can you keep order? Can you control the activity you are considering with the staff you have available? Perhaps you are considering a craft project. Your ratio between pupils and helpers will determine how complex of a project you might attempt. The more "on their own" students are, the simpler should be the project.

Then there are some practical logistics. Is the space available enough room for your chosen activity? It is challenging to have multiple learning stations in a small room. Do you have enough supplies/resources to keep everyone busy? It is difficult to keep children engaged if three of them have to share a crayon or paint brush. Are there enough helpers to do this smoothly? Some student-driven methods require significant supervision while others are easy to oversee with one or two leaders. Is the lighting sufficient for the artwork or reading project you want to assign? If children are going to be spread out, will they be able to hear you adequately?

How much time is available for this method? How long will it take to explain? How long will it take to perform? How long will it take to transition to the next activity? Are you likely to run out of time or have time left over? It is easy to assign time to most direct instruction. But the time to allow for high student involvement is harder to determine.

Of course, a very pertinent question is, what is the best (most effective) way to use your precious class time? That does not mean you have to choose the method that provides the greatest results, such as information communicated or highest percentage of participants. The best method is the one that achieves your purpose for that time slot.

Methods are a means to an end, not the end itself. It is unwise to become so method oriented that focus is drawn away from the lesson and the goals thereof. I am not speaking just of the students. Teachers risk the possibility of being so enraptured by methodology that the lesson becomes secondary. Avoid this.

What is the purpose of this method? Are you trying to gain or regain attention? Choose a method that takes very little time. Are you introducing the lesson or a new concept? You need a good interest getter. Is it time to test understanding or memory? A game, discussion, or some seat work might be in order. Do you need to illustrate or clarify a point? An object lesson or some other visual aid might be needed.

Once you've determined the purpose of the time slot, you can choose the best kinds of methods based upon the other criteria mentioned. One last question to ask yourself is, "Do I risk overusing this method, thus making it less effective and undesirable?" Teachers tend to have go-to tools and methods. There is nothing wrong with that. But you do need to be self-aware enough to recognize when you might be getting into a rut.

Choose your methods wisely and use them well.

Chapter Eighteen

General Age Characteristics

The better you understand the children to whom you minister, the better minister you can be. So, let's begin by considering some general characteristics of various ages of children. Some simple research will provide you with "official" charts and lists detailing characteristics of children by age. What follows is my distillation of some of that information seasoned with personal observation. Because I have almost no experience ministering to children age three and under, I will begin with the next group up.

Four and Five-Year-Olds

Physically, these children are experiencing rapid growth and exhibiting a high degree of energy. This tends to result in relatively short endurance. They get tired almost without warning. They can be going full bore one minute and whining the next. Their large muscles are growing, and they need to move. Being still (sitting) for long periods of time can be painful.

Eye-hand coordination and balance is beginning to improve, and is much better at age five than four. These children want to be independent with an "I can do it" attitude, but might still struggle with simple tasks. The ability to sing a tune is improving, but is often still off key.

Mentally, they are curious and love to learn. "Why" and "how" are becoming common questions. They are not adept at distinguishing between reality and fantasy. They find silly talk entertaining, especially when they do it.

Time is still a difficult concept. Yesterday, today and tomorrow are not so challenging. But referencing time further back or forward is not easily distinguishable. A memory from a year ago might be referred to as "the other day" while something two days before is called "a long time ago."

These children think literally. Symbolism and puns are meaningless. Five-year-olds are becoming more intellectual. But they often use words correctly by parroting rather than with true understanding. They enjoy listening to short stories.

Socially, they are beginning to make real friends. They tend to play in small groups, unkindly excluding others. They are still very "me" focused, but older ones are better at taking turns. Conflicts are frequent, but usually short lived.

They desire approval from adults. Some may test limits just to discover where they are. Once known, they seem to feel safe inside understood lines. They tend to be agreeable in an effort to conform and be accepted by leaders. They often try to imitate adults they admire.

Emotionally, four and five-year-olds are intense. Because much of the world is still very unfamiliar, they are marked by fearfulness. Curiously, these children often mirror the emotions of other children and leaders.

Spiritually, they are capable of simple trust in God and adults around them. They can recognize right and wrong but don't necessarily have a uniform sense of justice. They already share the common human trait of justifying themselves while judging others harshly.

While some children this age might be able to understand the gospel and accept responsibility as sinners, don't hurry them to make salvation decisions. Make sure any counseling done is in response to their initiating the conversation. Even then, just answer their questions one at a time. Do not force a full-fledged gospel witness on them. Be patient and trust God to provide wisdom in dealing with spiritual issues among these young people.

Six and Seven-Year-Olds
Physically, these youngsters are still very active. They love to move for movement's sake. While sitting still may not be painful, it is not desirable. Make sure they have plenty of opportunity to move about.

They are quite coordinated and able to perform most physical activities. Specific skills like those required in sports must be drilled and practiced to achieve proficiency. Their small muscle control and musical abilities have greatly improved.

Mentally, these children are eager to learn, having now a much better capacity to understand and to remember. This is a great time to begin Bible memorization. They have a firmer grasp on the difference between reality and fantasy. Chronology and geography are still difficult concepts. They don't distinguish between the Old and New Testaments well.

Six and seven-year-olds are still concrete thinkers. While they might enjoy object lessons, they don't easily get the point. They are reading pretty well, but it is risky to call on them to read out loud. They enjoy independent work and tend to be more careful as they get older. For example, a seven-year-old may take longer on a project than a six-year-old because the older child is more of a perfectionist.

Socially, they enjoy a club atmosphere and activities. They are much better with group activities. Friendships are important to them. But they are still very much focused on pleasing significant adults.

Emotionally, these children are not as explosive as when they were younger. But they can still break down and cry over what seems like a little thing to the teacher or parent. They are very self-conscious. They don't handle competition well because they want so badly to excel. They are poor losers.

Spiritually, many six and seven-year-olds are capable of understanding the gospel well enough to trust Christ as personal Savior. Again, let them take the initiative by asking questions. While their concept of God as a Spirit is still developing, they are capable of worship and growing in grace. You can tell how much you have impressed them with God's Word by letting them express themselves.

Eight and Nine-Year-Olds
Physically, eight and nine-year-olds are able to groom themselves (but boys don't see the need) and care for their own hygiene. They are physically developed enough to participate in sports in a meaningful way. Their skill sets and coordination are greatly enhanced. Lack of strength is their greatest physical weakness (pun intended).

Mentally, they can understand puns and enjoy humor. They are interested in how things work. Reading and writing skills are sufficient to communicate adequately. They can understand more complex mathematics, including reverse thinking skills. They are starting to take notice of current events. Attention span is markedly improved.

Socially, these children are beginning to separate by gender. They like to plan or at least be involved in planning activities. Sleepovers become common at this age, but they are still closely tethered to home and family.

Children this age are better able to handle conflict. They can resolve issues on their own, coming to an agreement with other children. They are beginning to enjoy competition without the need to always win or be the best.

Emotionally, eight and nine-year-olds tend to be anxious about getting good grades and being liked by authorities. Otherwise, this is a fairly tame stage of life emotionally. They are better able to resist the urge to express their emotions. They don't feel guilt quite as easily as one might hope.

Spiritually, this is a good age to come to Christ. Teachers can have more confidence that these children are old enough to understand and believe the gospel. They are still very much followers, so don't press for spiritual decisions or they may follow through just to please you or avoid conflict.

Ten and Eleven-Year-Olds
Physically, this is the age when the growth of boys and girls take different trajectories. Girls are at a growth spurt with puberty beginning or nearing. Boys often fall behind in height, only to catch up and pass in the early teen years. Puberty for most boys comes a couple of years later than girls.

Despite the fact that girls are often bigger, boys are usually rougher. This makes co-ed sporting activities less enjoyable for girls. The two genders grow apart as boys remain childish and girls are becoming more mature (they think). Girls have better small muscle control, but both can complain of growing pains, like muscle cramps.

Mentally, this age group is finally thinking more abstractly. They can keep track of a number of instructions (or steps) and appreciate timelines and maps. They are beginning to see things from more than one perspective and can start predicting the end of a course of action.

Puberty produces changes in the brain as well as in the body. These changes are allowing children to think more like adults, but without the vast experience to put such thinking into context. They still tend to be two-dimensional thinkers: right and wrong, good and bad, etc. They have great memory skills which can frustrate adults who make casual promises. They will remind you of what you said.

Socially, ten and eleven-year-olds are becoming more influenced by peers. They get busy with outside activities, which often encourages more independence from the immediate family. As mentioned before, boys and girls tend to disassociate for the most part. Despite that, many of them experiment with boyfriend/girlfriend relationships.

Because of physical changes occurring or on the horizon, they can become awkward and insecure. They are drawn to "heroes." They admire people who can do things they wish they could do. Athletes and entertainers are on top of that list. Wise guidance toward Biblical role models is needed.

Emotionally, they vacillate between being confident and insecure. They are loyal to people who they believe care about them. Remarkably, fear continues to be a major emotion. It just focuses on new things. Juniors are developing a strong sense of guilt. They recognize their own wrongs and sin and cannot easily excuse them.

ATTENTION PLEASE

Children this age who have experienced major life changes like divorce can be distant emotionally. Many children with difficult home lives are aggressive. These emotional walls are designed to protect against further pain and suffering. For some, the harsh realities of life come way too early.

Spiritually, healthy older children are fully able to understand the gospel and trust Christ as Savior. Most children who have been in an evangelistic church for a long time have done so by this age. This is a time to help them develop a more personal walk with God. Help them understand that Christianity is not about a list of rules, but a relationship with God, through Christ.

They are old enough to not only participate in worship, but to help plan worship events. They are eager to take active part and volunteer to serve. Provide ways for them to serve others in your church and outside, if possible. Let them help set up chairs, distribute bulletins, or help younger children with projects. Let them worship and serve.

Zero in on the age group to whom you minister. Understanding them will provide you with the potential to truly make an impact in their lives.

Chapter Nineteen

Final Thoughts

There are many aspects of the teaching/learning process that affect attention and/or are influenced by attention. Most of us in Christian children's ministry would be hard pressed to read a textbook on educational psychology because it simply is not interesting to the average volunteer. And yet, there are some valuable insights that can benefit every serious children's worker.

With that introduction, I offer the following hodgepodge of educational tidbits in distilled form.

Expectation

So, how did you feel about the opening statement of this chapter? Was it disappointing? Did I come across as unconvinced that what was to follow would be worth your time? Probably.

Our expectation greatly affects the result of our activity, in this case, teaching. You've probably heard or read about an educational experiment that involved two groups of similar children. One teacher was told her class was the worst of the worst. The other teacher was told she had the cream of the crop. Student test scores were very revealing. The "bad kids" scored much lower than the "good kids."

In truth, the two classes consisted of similarly skilled and tempered children. The only difference between the two classes was the teacher's expectation. The teacher who expects great things from her students graded higher. The other graded lower because of her predisposition.

If you expect teaching will be difficult, it will be. If you think you won't be able to handle problems, you'll be right. If you are excited about what God will do in the lives of your students, you will not be disappointed.

Motivation

There are two main types of motivation. Intrinsic motivation causes someone to learn out of personal desire or interest. Whether it is based upon curiosity, self-preservation, or something else, this form finds learning to be its own reward. Extrinsic motivation involves an external reason for doing something. This is commonly the promise of reward or threat of punishment. Learning that comes as a result of extrinsic motivation is less desirable and effective.

As teachers, we can and should try to motivate our students to be involved in the learning process. But ultimately, if God is going to work, there must be a transition from our presentation of extrinsic motivations to the child personally desiring to walk with God. Only God can do that. But teachers must be aware of the need for that dynamic. We try to motivate our students to become self-motivated.

We should be helping children discover that knowing and loving God its own reward.

Curiosity

One of the great influencers of interest is curiosity. Children very much enjoy novelty. They like surprises. Unexpected things will arouse your pupils' attention. Older children especially appreciate puzzling things. They like to figure stuff out. You can engage them with an activity that helps them discover truth more than you can by just telling them what they need to know.

Questions, riddles and intrigue are enticing. Help your students make their own discoveries of God and truth. Some human needs, like hunger, decrease once satisfied. When other "needs" like increased knowledge/understanding are satisfied, they are magnified by a desire for more. Follow the old "salting the horse" adage, don't give children a drink of truth until you've given them a thirst for it.

Excitement

At the risk of sounding carnal, I implore you to be exciting; or at least create excitement. Your class time does not have to emulate a circus environment. But it should exude an obvious amount of energy. Children bore easily.

I've told groups of Christian educators, "You can bore children with history if necessary. You can bore them when you teach language skills if you must. You can bore them when explaining concepts of math if you'd like. Even bore them with science. But never, ever bore children with the Bible.

Among all the things your teaching might accomplish, one of the most important is this: How you teach the Bible will greatly influence your students' attitude about God, Scripture and church. Do all you can to be the teacher whose life and ministry brings children to Christ.

I have tried to convey to you the importance of gaining and maintaining attention for effective teaching. I've encouraged you to fill your teaching toolbox with methods and knowledge that will help you communicate. Let me close with this important caveat.

God alone changes hearts. Become the best teacher you can be, using the best tools you can gather. But don't expect them to change lives. You must develop the relationship with God that you are teaching your children to pursue. You must rely on Him to do the work while you serve as one of His instruments.

God bless your ministry to children.

Appendix

Following, are three of the songs mentioned in chapter twelve. These include the lyrics and melody only. You are free to use whatever accompaniment is compatible with your ministry.

This material is protected by copy write, so you may not publish any of this music without expressed written permission. However, the owner of this book may print enough copies to use within your own children's ministry.

You can also access these songs and other materials at our website, www.SundayTeachers.com.

Don't Quit

Jeff Welch

God told Mo-ses to lead his peo - ple out, lead his peo - ple out of
God told Mo-ses to warn that He would send, warn that He would send some
God tells us to-day, al - ways to o - bey, al - ways to o - bey His

E - gypt land. He told Pha - raoh, "Let my peo - ple go!"
migh - ty plagues. Af - ter num - ber ten made ol' Pha - raoh bend.
ho - ly word. Al - though do - ing right may take all your might,

Pha - raoh just said no to the Lord's com-mand. Don't quit! Ne-ver give up.
God won in the end, and His peo - ple saved.
you will win the fight, trust-ing in the Lord.

Ne-ver give in. Ne-ver give out. Don't quit, what - ev - er the cost, what-

ev - er the loss. Ne - ver give up.

Armor of God

Jeff Welch

Put on the ar - mor, the ar - mor of God. March down the path that the

faith - ful have trod. Put on the ar - mor, re - sist e - v'ry foe.

We will win the bat - tle. The Bi - ble tells me so. Put on the belt of

truth, and the breast - plate of right - eous - ness. Pre - pare your feet to spread the

gos - pell of our Lord. Tak - ing the shield of faith. Wear - ing sal - va - tion's

hel - met. Bear - ing the word of God, the Spi - rit's sword.

117

Lord, Speak to Me

Jeff Welch

I close my eyes, I bow my head. And thank you for the blood you
So ma - ny times I've failed you Lord. So ma - ny times your will ig -

shed, to give me life when I was dead in tres - pass - es and sin Lord,
nored. How of - ten I ne - glet your word to make room for my sin. I

speak to me, I hum - bly pray. I need to hear from you to - day. Then
now re - pent on bend - ed knees. I want no more my - self to please. I'm

grant me pow - er to o - bey. And thus, the vic - t'ry win.
rest - ing in the One who frees, and clean - ses from with - in.

Other books by Jeff Welch

Feed My Lambs: Become a Teacher that Makes a Difference equips teachers of children in Christian ministry to change how they teach so that they can teach for change. This book is a distillation of the material that Jeff teaches in colleges, camps and churches around the world. It will help you become the best teacher you can be.

Christ For Kids: Changing How We Counsel Children About Salvation teaches you how to share the gospel with children in a way that helps them avoid doubting their salvation experience later in life. In it, Jeff explains the common reasons young people doubt their salvation and how you can counsel them more adequately.

The Gospel For Children: 31 devotions to help children understand salvation and trust Christ with confidence provides parents, teachers and ministry leaders with a resource to help youngsters understand important truths related to the gospel. Adults can read this book to young people or let older children read it for themselves. Because it includes a lot of Scripture, this book is available in two editions; the Authorized King James Version, and easy to read English Standard Version.

Made in the USA
Columbia, SC
05 February 2020